Material Strategies

Also in the Architecture Brief series:

Architects Draw
Sue Ferguson Gussow
ISBN 978-1-56898-740-8

Architectural Lighting:
Designing with Light and Space
Herve Descottes, Cecilia E. Ramos
ISBN 978-1-56898-938-9

Architectural Photography the Digital Way
Gerry Kopelow
ISBN 978-1-56898-697-5

Building Envelopes:
An Integrated Approach
Jenny Lovell
ISBN 978-1-56898-818-4

Digital Fabrications:
Architectural and Material Techniques
Lisa Iwamoto
ISBN 978-1-56898-790-3

Ethics for Architects:
50 Dilemmas of Professional Practice
Thomas Fisher
ISBN 978-1-56898-946-4

Model Making
Megan Werner
ISBN 978-1-56898-870-2

Old Buildings, New Designs:
Architectural Transformations
Charles Bloszies
ISBN 978-1-61689-035-3

Philosophy for Architects
Branko Mitrović
ISBN 978-1-56898-994-5

Sustainable Design:
A Critical Guide
David Bergman
ISBN 978-1-56898-941-9

Urban Composition:
Developing Community through Design
Mark C. Childs
ISBN 978-1-61689-052-0

Writing about Architecture:
Mastering the Language of Buildings and Cities
Alexandra Lange
ISBN 978-1-61689-053-7

MATERIAL STRATEGIES

INNOVATIVE APPLICATIONS IN ARCHITECTURE

Blaine Brownell

Princeton Architectural Press, New York

To Nancie and Michael Warner, my first teachers of art and building.

Published by
Princeton Architectural Press
37 East 7th Street
New York, NY 10003

Visit our website at www.papress.com

Editor: Linda Lee
Designer: Paul Wagner

Special thanks to: Bree Anne Apperley, Sara Bader, Nicola Bednarek Brower,
Janet Behning, Fannie Bushin, Megan Carey, Carina Cha, Tom Cho, Russell Fernandez,
Jan Haux, Felipe Hoyos, Jennifer Lippert, Gina Morrow, John Myers, Katharine Myers,
Margaret Rogalski, Dan Simon, Andrew Stepanian, Joseph Weston, and Deb Wood
of Princeton Architectural Press —Kevin C. Lippert, publisher

Library of Congress
Cataloging-in-Publication Data
Brownell, Blaine, 1970–
Material strategies : innovative applications in architecture /
Blaine Brownell. — 1st ed.
    p.   cm. — (Architecture briefs)
Includes bibliographical references and index.
ISBN 978-1-56898-986-0 (alk. paper)
1. Building materials—Technological innovations. 2. Architecture—
Technological innovations—Case studies. I. Title.
TA403.6.B76 2012
721'.04—dc23
                    2011019044

MINERAL   15

CONCRETE   41

WOOD   61

METAL   83

GLASS   105

PLASTIC   127

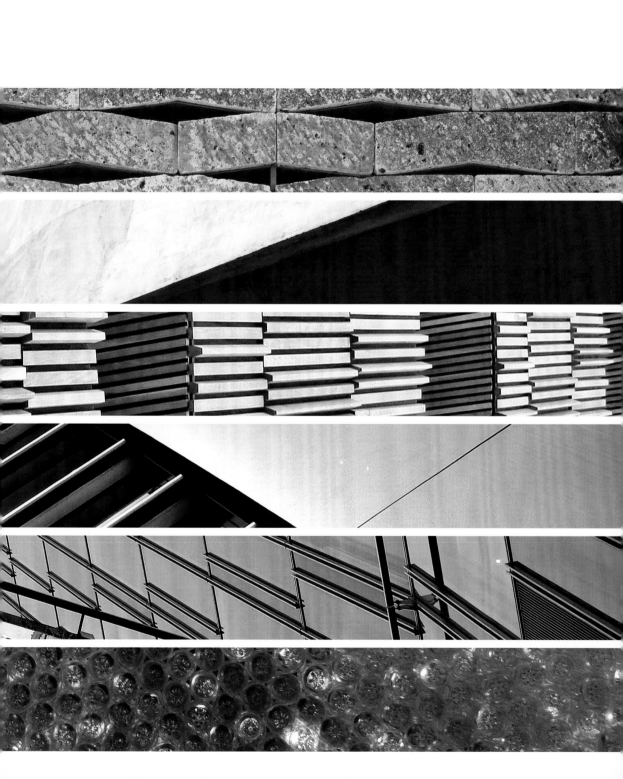

Introduction

Architecture is born out of the shrewd alignment of concept and matter. The product of what Louis Kahn termed "the measurable and the unmeasurable," architecture is the fulfillment of a spatial premise by way of material substance.[1] Throughout history architecture has been shaped by the continual transformation of material technologies and application methods. Its course of development is inseparable from the shifting terrain of technology and the social effects that result. This intrinsic alignment with change—whether from a welcomed or critical perspective—reveals the extent to which architecture is inherently tied to material innovation.

In his assessment of canonical twentieth-century works of architecture, historian Richard Weston states that "the bias has been toward those [buildings] that were innovative—stylistically, technically, or programmatically—and especially those that significantly affected the course of architecture."[2] On one hand, new products and processes have transformed architecture by enabling alternative construction techniques and novel spatial possibilities. On the other hand, the architect's utilization of materials in unexpected ways has demonstrated architecture's capacity to inspire new growth in construction-related industries as well as stimulate cultural change. Both tendencies demonstrate the extent to which the innovative application of materials has been vital to the advancement of architecture.

Motivations

Innovation is motivated by a variety of factors. The recognition of an acute economic, social or environmental need can spur novel solutions, as seen in the development of the skyscraper in land-starved cities in the 1880s, modern social housing during the 1920s urban expansion, or superinsulated buildings during the 1970s oil crisis. The expansion of new technologies beyond their original fields can also spark innovation, such as materials developed for military or aerospace uses that find their way to the consumer marketplace.

Presently, the world faces a series of fundamental challenges that define a new context for architecture. The scale and pace of environmental, technological, and social change today is remarkable. Population growth and accelerating urban migrations outpace the replenishment capacity of the earth's resources. Global warming, desertification, and eutrophication portend ominous climate transformations. At the same time, the rate and number of new technologies have recently exploded. Vastly more new products are available for architecture than in the previous history of building construction, and the rapid deployment of low-cost communication and computer technologies has enabled increasing populations to participate in a broader global conversation, propagating the visual potency and cultural-shaping capacity of design.[3] The result of these changes presents an unrivaled set of complexities for architects as well as opportunities in architecture, which—since buildings consume nearly half of all energy and resources—will inevitably evolve accordingly.

It is not sufficient for architecture to respond to this new environmental, technological, and social context with modest, shortsighted changes. Anticipating our current situation, Buckminster Fuller proposed a concept he called the "world game," which claims that a global population with access to sophisticated technologies and robust data about world resources and their distribution would make beneficial choices for humanity as well as the environment.[4] Today, architect Bill McDonough and partner chemist Michael Braungart call not only for increased access to information for the global population but also for a greater level of action. They claim that incremental progress is inadequate for meeting current challenges and advocate the initiation of "the next industrial revolution" in which we rethink the buildings and products we make as well as the methods used to make them.[5]

In order to fulfill this goal, architects must replace status-quo thinking with enlightened proposals for alternative methods and manifestations of design. Supporting the idea that shifting one's expectations exposes the limitations of traditional practices and environments, media scholar Marshall McLuhan championed the transformation of the environment itself into a work of art.[6] He advocated the pursuit of "hidden" or "counter-environments" that directly thwart the desensitizing, limited nature of conventional environments in order to increase the authenticity of perception. McLuhan warns us of the danger in upholding conventional order: "Our typical response to a disrupting new technology is to re-create the old environment instead of heeding the new opportunities of the new environment. Failure to notice the new opportunities is also failure to understand the new powers....This failure leaves us in the role of mere automata."[7]

The Knowledge Gap

Despite the broadly appreciated need to transcend convention, specific methodologies for achieving material innovation in design are rarely taught in academia or practice. In architectural curricula, material education typically occurs within a building-technology sequence, in which students are given information about basic material properties and conventional approaches. Students are exposed to canonical precedents but are not often taught the significance of the particular material achievements of those examples. Learning the foundations is necessary to articulate a more sophisticated vocabulary; however, the rote following of traditional practices practically ensures an unremarkable result. Architectural practice is worse: in the majority of offices, there is no established discipline or method for material innovation—despite the widespread belief in its importance. Moreover, material methods are often discussed purely within a technological context, although the implications of material decisions also affect a broad set of conceptual, theoretical, and design conditions.

Disruptive Innovation

In order to understand the nature of material innovation, we must give it a more precise definition. McLuhan's articulation of "disruptive technology"— an expression used by and further developed by technology theorist Clayton Christensen—describes a new product or material that displaces an old one unexpectedly.[8] Disruptive technologies exhibit competitive advantages over so-called sustaining technologies that offer small, incremental growth. Although necessarily novel and unproven when first introduced, disruptive technologies often supersede existing technologies rapidly. Light-emitting-diode (LED) lighting—one example of a disruptive technology—has quickly emerged as a durable, low-energy alternative to many types of incandescent and fluorescent lighting.

In a similar way, a *disruptive application* is an unexpected replacement of a conventional design or construction practice with a new one. While disruptive technology generally refers to a product or material, a disruptive application considers a more complex system or physical assembly—such as a building—as well as its larger cultural and environmental context. An application is not only considered disruptive in the result it produces but also in the methods used to achieve the result—such as in the robotic fabrication of brick panels instead of traditional hand-laying. Disruptive applications may employ disruptive technologies, or they may exhibit unanticipated uses of conventional technologies. Both disruptive technologies and applications are defined by the fulfillment of the unexpected: an aberration or mutation that upsets and displaces the status quo within conventional systems of praxis.

Le Corbusier championed the necessary pursuit of material innovation in *Towards a New Architecture*: "It is our business to use the materials and constructional methods to our hand, not, of course, blindly, but with a constant endeavor to improve them.... An architecture of our own age is slowly but surely shaping itself; its main lines become more and more evident."⁹ Ever since Le Corbusier declared "Architecture or Revolution" in *Towards a New Architecture*, architects have speculated about the role of innovation in design. *Innovation* is, after all, a vague term that implies novelty and positive change.

Recent interest, however, has inspired the establishment of more precise definitions of the word in the fields of engineering and economics. According to polymer chemist Dirk Funhoff, "innovation is the establishment in the marketplace of a new technical or organizational idea, not just the invention of such."¹⁰ In *The Nature of Technology*, economist W. Brian Arthur describes mechanisms of innovation as "radically novel technologies being brought into being by the process of invention [and] whole bodies of technology emerging, building out over time, and creatively transforming the industries that encounter them."¹¹ While economists and engineers have developed sophisticated methods for improving product performance and manufacturing methods (technology), less is known about how to engage positive cognitive and emotional responses in users (design). Although design is commonly described as a method to solve problems, it is also a critical means of shifting expectations. In the book *Design-Driven Innovation*, business scholar Roberto Verganti emphasizes the transformative role of design, describing design-driven innovation as "the radical innovation of meaning."¹²

Strategies

Taking a cue from Verganti, we may posit that disruptive applications in architecture evoke transformational shifts in meaning. Architect Jun Aoki describes this phenomenon in terms of a "material code": "A material is perceived according to a code—a social code. And so we can manipulate the code itself."¹³ This recodification may be applied in architecture at different physical scales, and the adjustment of meaning can engender a variety of

specific effects. This process requires a knowledge of the anticipated audience and its collective set of prior experiences—a mnemonic framework that designer and critic Kenya Hara terms "information architecture."¹⁴ By appreciating an observer's expected means of engaging architecture based on established habits, the architect can develop novel experiences that intensify one's impression, thereby broadening his or her set of experiences. In this way, architects are not merely manipulators of form, but orchestrators of information.

In examining a broad range of historical precedents and contemporary projects that recalibrate material meaning, I have observed that the most influential works of architecture adhere to five strategies, which I have named as follows: push limits, assimilate, reveal-conceal, surprise, and edit. Although these are general categories that often overlap, they reveal insights into the art and science of material innovation.

Push Limits: Because of the common focus on standard practices in building construction, architecture needs to push existing limits. According to architect Takaharu Tezuka, it is imperative that architects seek to expand the boundaries of architecture to avoid delivering predictable designs.¹⁵ The limits to be redefined are often structural but may also involve technical, formal, environmental, and cultural aspects. Typically presumed to be fixed, limits can often be malleable with adequate research and testing. Architect Stan Allen reminds us that "in any profession there are those who operate by rote, at minimal professional standards, and there are those capable of imagination, invention, and creative thinking. In short, those working to push the limits of the discipline."¹⁶

Assimilate: Assimilation entails synthesis between constituent parts (often accepted as discrete in architectural circles) to make an integrated whole and intentionally blurs boundaries between domains—such as inside and outside; facade and structure; building and furniture; architecture and engineering; architecture and landscape; or wall, floor, and ceiling. Assimilation is distinct from "integrated design," a popular phrase that refers to the seamless coordination of the physical components of a building. Design integrity should be a given in architecture, although integrated design typically results in the preservation of the individuality of components, such as structural and mechanical systems. Assimilation, by contrast, seeks integration by unifying concepts rather than by bringing together individual parts.

Reveal-Conceal: Adolf Loos once quoted Louis Sullivan as having said that "it could only benefit us if for a time we were to abandon ornament and concentrate entirely on the erection of buildings that were finely shaped and charming in their sobriety."[17] This sentiment undoubtedly influenced Loos's 1908 article "Ornament and Crime," which eschewed the use of excess patterning and material. The International Style, likewise, promoted the elimination of surplus materials and coatings in favor of material honesty— a legacy that continues to influence contemporary design. Interestingly, the reduction of excess material often results in "zero detailing," a process that requires the suppression of certain materials or systems to maximize clarity and simplicity. This method results in hiding some physical components that would typically be exposed, such as window framing, in order to reduce visual distractions. In this way, illusion is often given comparable treatment to raw honesty. Moreover, because zero detailing requires more effort to design and construct, craft becomes essential for the execution of unusual material conditions. Architecture thus requires careful consideration of what is and is not expressed, and every joint, corner, and material intersection is subject to scrutiny.

Surprise: Architecture must surprise. This is the inherent nature of making counter-environments— works that elevate consciousness. Innovation entails the defiance of convention and often involves the exploitation of new technologies. The effect may be shocking or barely perceptible, large or small, solemn or humorous. Architect Kengo Kuma counteracts conventional practices in architecture by upsetting traditional expectations of structure, materials, and light. "Reality is only truly perceived in the presence of some unreality," says Kuma, who believes that if design "is a little unreal, there is a little bit of a surprise. If there is no surprise with something, it is not real, because it goes unnoticed. It might as well not exist."[18] By upending our expectations, Kuma awakens our consciousness from the paralyzing realm of the everyday.

Edit: Architecture requires a clear purpose and must be executed with conviction and precision. This goal demands thoughtful consideration of every space, system, and material in a project—especially elements introduced by consultants and the contractor, which must be closely monitored for the purposes of design integration. Editing demands the elimination of unnecessary components and typically recommends a limited material palette. While the reveal-conceal strategy focuses primarily on architectural tectonics, editing considers the entirety of a building as well as its site. Editing seeks to refine, navigating a precarious line between the simple and the simplistic—to clarify without being routine or uninspired. The desired outcome is one of "simplexity," a condition that is simultaneously intelligible and intelligent, which addresses the inevitable complexities of practice with straightforward rules.[19] In order to realize authoritative and inspired executions, editing requires the architect to establish simple rules that can be understood and followed by the entire design team.

Effects

To employ these strategies successfully, architects must be conscious of the particular results they will produce. This recodification may be applied in architecture at different physical scales, and the adjustment of meaning can engender visual, operational, behavioral, cultural, and/or environmental effects. Changes in meaning in any combination of these five dimensions often occur simultaneously in architecture and may evoke a range of responses—from subtle or startling—in the occupant or user of a building. The larger the number of effects involved, the greater the overall influence.

Visual effects relate to what Le Corbusier termed the "plastic invention" of the discipline.[20] They incorporate the use of unexpected forms, systems, or technologies, and include the interplay of light and material. This is the most direct and accessible dimension, involving a literal recoding of material meaning. Projects may adjust meaning with visually arresting features, such as the protruding acrylic rods of Heatherwick Studio's Seed Cathedral (see pages 146–49). They may also exhibit more subtle shifts in material manipulations, such as with the "wallpaper" brick employed by Jun Aoki & Associates in the Aomori Museum of Art (see page 23). Architects consider the specific response that a visual effect will inspire in an audience. James Carpenter's gravity-defying glass bridge (see pages 114–15), for example, impresses immediate awe to a broad audience, while Zhu Jianping's clever use of wheat tile as a replacement for conventional ceramics in the 2049 Pavilion (see pages 80–81) demands more careful observation.

Operational effects entail a change in the functional services and systems of architecture. Disruptive technologies may be employed to maximize occupant comfort, improve environmental performance, or provide a function previously absent. Examples of operational effects include the use of building integrated photovoltaics to harness solar energy and convert it to nighttime illumination in Simone Giostra & Partners' GreenPix project (see pages 122–25) and the incorporation of phase-change materials to reduce surface temperature fluctuations in 3xn's Learning from Nature Pavilion (see pages 140–41). Depending on the scale of implementation,

operational innovations may also instill behavioral and cultural effects (discussed below) by transforming lifestyles through enhanced convenience. Modern plumbing, for example, is an operational innovation that has prompted these effects in a significant way.

Behavioral effects concern the alteration of human behavior. This dimension is realized through the reformulation of program, circulation, or multisensory conditions within architecture. A behavioral effect relates primarily to the scale of the individual or small group, as it considers direct physical relationships between people and buildings. Philip Johnson's Glass House (see page 108) and Mies van der Rohe's Farnsworth House (see page 87), for example, both dissolve the visual boundaries between interior and exterior, laying bare the intimate activities of the domestic realm and influencing occupants to behave in a more public manner. As architectural historian Elizabeth Cromley relates, "[Edith] Farnsworth complained that she was often being looked at by others both inside and outside her home…She wanted distinct bedrooms to preserve some privacy, but Mies had designed her house with sleeping areas, not enclosed rooms."[21] The glass enclosure, in this case, psychologically affected and altered the behavior of the building occupant.

Other types of material application exert direct physical influences. The three-dimensional stacking of wood timbers in Sou Fujimoto's Final Wooden House (see pages 72–73), for example, creates a space delineated by terracelike constructions with multiple implied functions. Individual choice rather than preconditioned experience determines the occupant's use of these staggered timbers as stairs, work surfaces, seating, or storage—the house inspires a kind of flexible and open-ended behavioral opportunism in response to the physical artifact of the building.

Cultural effects are behavioral effects at the larger scale of communities and societies: behavioral effects often produce temporary results, and cultural effects result in abiding transformations. Cultural effects indicate significant change brought about by either the widespread adoption of a material application that influences human behavior or by a particular building that exerts a meaningful cultural influence far beyond its own physical territory. The former condition is exemplified in the development and proliferation of the skyscraper. Originally made possible by the invention of the steel frame and the elevator, the skyscraper facilitated the vertical stacking and densification of commercial activities and human settlements, radically transforming urban form as a result (see Shreve, Lamb & Harmon's Empire State Building, page 86). The latter condition is represented by 86 attractions such as Renzo Piano and Richard Rogers's Centre Georges Pompidou (see page 87) and Frank Gehry's Guggenheim Museum Bilbao (see page 88), which have both captured the popular imagination, inspired changes in future building practices, and stimulated their local economies (this phenomenon is also known as "the Bilbao effect").

Environmental effects address the repercussions of material applications on the environment. The scale of environmental effects ranges from macro to micro, addressing metropolitan development as well as human-scaled installations. Because industrialization has engendered many negative environmental consequences, current applications must disrupt the postindustrial status quo and improve the poor environmental record of conventional practices. One approach is the architectural integration of renewable-power technologies to decrease a building's energy demands, as seen in Inaba Electric Works' Eco-Curtain wind-harnessing facade (see page 91). Another example is the selection of environmentally friendly alternatives to conventional materials, such as the cross-laminated timber used for the structure of Waugh Thistleton Architects' Stadthaus (see page 70–71), which has a significantly lower carbon footprint than conventional concrete or steel.

Explanation of the Book

Material Strategies is a primer that addresses how materials have been used as well as "misused" throughout architectural history, with a focus on recent projects. It aims to provide insights regarding emerging material trends as well as the creative implementation of materials. The book is organized into a concise set of chapters based on fundamental material categories—mineral, concrete, wood, metal, glass, and plastic. The introduction to each chapter describes the basic history of the material and its importance to architecture, offering a summary of previous building innovations and their technological as well as cultural influence. Each chapter also contains discussions regarding current environmental challenges and their future ramifications, recent disruptive technologies and their preliminary manifestations, as well as a series of disruptive applications exemplified by recent pioneering buildings. Comprehensively documented architectural case studies, presented at the end of each chapter, focus on the significance of their contributions to the evolution of a particular material and demonstrate the successful realization of material-based innovation.

Material Strategies acknowledges exceptional works within the established architectural canon, with a focus on contemporary projects because of the creative ways in which they contribute to present-day circumstances. In addition, the unusual approaches to material apparent in these case studies speak to the multiple dimensions of architectural research and scholarship—technique, theory, aesthetics, and environmental performance, for example—as opposed to a more typical approach in which preference is given to only one aspect. *Material Strategies* was written with the intention of educating and inspiring a broad audience about the fundamental importance of—and methods inherent in—pursuing material innovation in architecture.

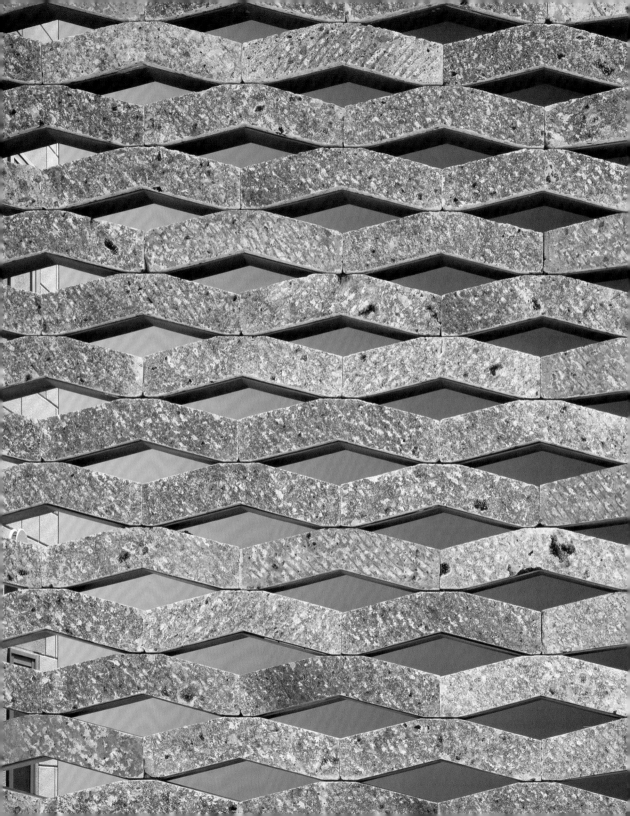

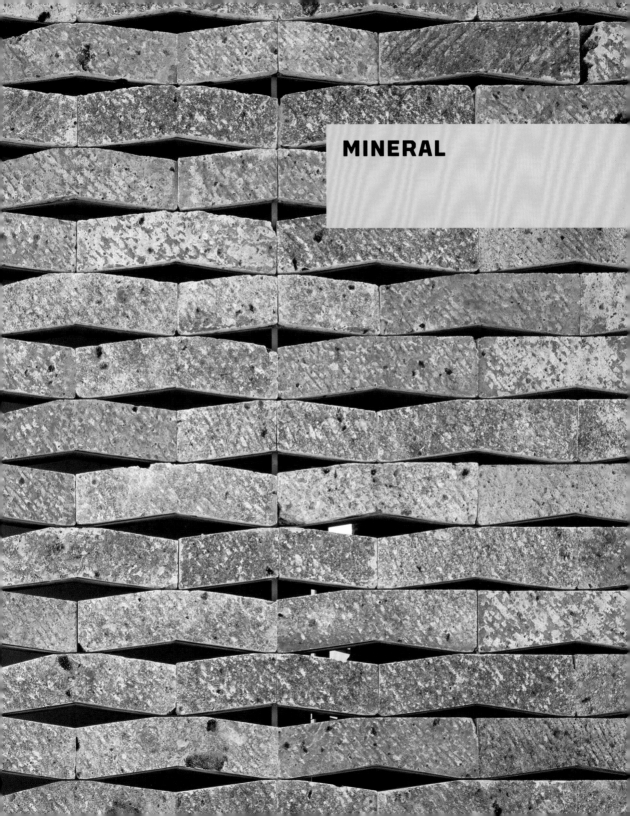

MINERAL

MINERAL

PAGES 14-15: Kengo Kuma & Associates, Chokkura Plaza and Shelter, Tochigi, Japan, 2006, exterior detail of Oya stone

Soft tissue (gels and aerosols, muscle and nerve) reigned supreme until 500 million years ago. At that point, some of the conglomerations of fleshy matter-energy that made up life underwent a sudden mineralization, and a new material for constructing living creatures emerged: bone....The human endoskeleton was one of the many products of that ancient mineralization.... About eight thousand years ago, human populations began mineralizing again when they developed an urban exoskeleton: bricks of sun-dried clay became the building materials for their homes, which in turn surrounded and were surrounded by stone monuments and defensive walls. – Manuel De Landa

Earthen minerals were some of the first materials that early hominids used to make shelter and tools. Many ancient myths and religions associated earth and stone with human flesh and bone, respectively—minerals of varying consistency were seen as symbolically connected to the body and its dual characteristics of suppleness and fortitude. Archaeological records indicate active manipulation of stone during the prehistoric period known as the Stone Age, which accounted for more than 99 percent of human existence. The transition from the Stone Age into the Copper and Bronze ages roughly marks the beginning of recorded history.

Loam, stone, and ceramics—the primary materials considered in this chapter—were fundamental to the genesis of civilization, and they gave physical form and order to the first cities. Because of their compressive strength, these materials were appropriate for the thick-walled, low-slung structures that emerged as layers of earth were laid and compacted to make the first load-bearing walls. For millennia this striated architecture signified weight, presence, and longevity. [FIGS. 1-3]

Today the use of the load-bearing wall has all but disappeared in industrialized nations and has been replaced by frame construction with applied skins. The persistence of earthen materials in contemporary building despite this transformation is a testament to their powerful legacy. The current applications of stone and brick are generally suspended or self-supporting surfaces over skeletal frames—a perverse transformation from their original use. However, both the broad availability of many mineral resources and the perseverance of stone and ceramics as architectural membranes suggest continued importance of earthen materials in building construction.

Composition

Rock is the product of the crystallization of liquid magma. There are three types of rock, classified by their formation process: igneous rock is the "original rock," formed directly from liquid magma;

TOP, LEFT TO RIGHT:
FIG. 1: Postumius, Temple of Castor and Pollux, Rome, 484 BCE

FIG. 2: Teotihuacán, Mexico, 100-250 BCE, detail of platforms along the Avenue of the Dead
FIG. 3: Chángchéng (Great Wall), Badaling, China, 1368-1644

BOTTOM, LEFT TO RIGHT:
FIG. 4: Ryoanji, Kyoto, Japan, late-fifteenth century, detail of earth wall

FIG. 5: Yong He Gong (Lama Temple), Beijing, China, 1694, detail of ornamental tile

17

MINERAL

 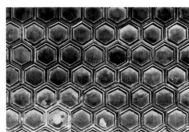

sedimentary rock is made of particles from rocks (sediment) that have been deposited in layers and solidified by a physical and chemical process called diagenesis; and metamorphic rock is igneous or sedimentary rock that has been transformed via intense heat and pressure. The most common types of stones used for building include granite and basalt (igneous), sandstone and limestone (sedimentary), and marble, slate, and gneiss (metamorphic).

Loam consists of equal parts clay, silt, and sand. Clay, made of decomposed rock and of finer particles than the other two, acts as the binder for the other materials. Loam is a relatively weak material, which can be strengthened by adding gravel and organic reinforcing materials, such as straw. For added durability, it is typically tamped or compressed to make rammed earth, or *pisé*. Loam is typically employed in one of two forms: as prefabricated bricks and blocks or as loose bulk material for in-situ castings. [**FIG. 4**]

A ceramic is a nonmetallic material, such as clay, that is transformed by heat into a stonelike substance. The clay typically used to make ceramics consists of hydrous aluminum silicate compounds derived from feldspar-rich rocks, as well as mica, calcite, iron oxides, and quartz.[1] The physical properties of ceramics depend on the kind of clay—kaolinite, montmorillonite-smectite, and illite are the three most common types used. Firing temperature is also an influential factor, and stronger, more refined ceramics require higher temperatures. Clayware and stoneware have low firing temperatures (900–1300°C), while porcelain and oxidized ceramics are fired at higher temperatures (1300–2100°C).[2] Common ceramic elements used in building construction include bricks, pipes, tiles, and ceramic panels. [**FIG. 5**]

History

Earthen materials were critical to the origins of technology. The development of stone tools and pottery, as well as the construction of early shelters, occurred during the Stone Age (2.9 MYA–6500 BCE), the first human epoch. Megalithic monuments, such as stone circles, dolmens, and cairns, constructed of large, regularly shaped stones are enduring reminders of tombs and sacred sites of the period—Stonehenge (3100–1600 BCE) being the most familiar example.

FIG. 6: Imhotep, Pyramid of Djoser, Egypt, twenty-seventh century BCE

FIG. 7: Stephansdom Cathedral, Vienna, Austria, 1160

FIG. 8: Antonio Gaudí, Casa Batllo, Barcelona, Spain, 1877, detail of trencadís tilework on parapet

FIG. 9: Adolf Loos, Loos House, Vienna, Austria, 1910, detail of marble base

The first stepped pyramid, the Pyramid of Djoser, was built in Egypt around 2600 BCE for Pharaoh Djoser. [**FIG. 6**] Imhotep, considered to be the first architect, designed and oversaw the pyramid's construction and used rough-cut Tura limestone blocks for the enclosure wall, colonnaded entrance, and pyramid. The use of limestone was a much more durable alternative to the use of mud brick, a material common to early Nile river–valley societies and an expedient resource for settlement building, also used in earlier Egyptian tombs.

Djoser exhibits one of the first known uses of the architectural column. The colonnade at the Pyramid of Djoser consists of pillars carved to resemble bundled plants—one of the first instances of architectural transubstantiation of wood into stone. The Greeks continued this approach, developing proportion-based systems and techniques that transformed stone used in building from coarse blocks into refined, specialized modules resembling abstracted components of trees and plants.

The Greeks also further developed ceramic materials—which offer good compressive strength and moisture resistance—from the early pottery-based tiles and fired bricks used in Egypt and Mesopotamia (as early as 4000 BCE) to modular building elements such as roof tiles designed to overlap like fish scales to direct the flow of water (800 BCE). (The word *ceramics* derives from the Greek word *keramos*, meaning fired earth.) The Romans further augmented ceramic technologies in their extensive use of brick, which was often applied to walls of concrete.

Stone technology achieved its apex during the Middle Ages with the construction of soaring Gothic churches. [**FIG. 7**] Stonemasons developed increasingly sophisticated vaulting and buttressing technology that allowed stone to reach unprecedented heights, conveying an uncanny lightness and delicacy despite its heavy weight. Although later industrialization enabled greater control in the manufacturing and distribution of stone and ceramics, the arrival of frame construction in the nineteenth century rendered the load-bearing application of these materials obsolete.

Modern Precedents

Despite the change in load-management practices, stone and ceramics are still widely used. After the ascendance of steel, concrete, and wood stud framing systems during the nineteenth century, earthen materials were applied in veneer form—layered with other materials to create architectural surfaces with durability and presence. Antonio Gaudí's constructions of elaborate mosaics using broken clay tiles (called *trencadís*) are exuberant examples of these types of embellished surfaces. [**FIG. 8**] Adolf Loos's use of highly figured Cipollino marble in the facade of his Loos House (1910) in Vienna achieves a flamboyance with the material itself. [**FIG. 9**] Adhering to precise geometries, the tile cladding on Jørn Utzon's Sydney Opera House (1973) roof shells is another example of the maturation of earthen veneers.

For Uruguayan engineer Eladio Dieste, brick had a more significant role than as decorative veneer. He selected the material as the primary building block for

TOP, LEFT TO RIGHT:

FIG. 10: Eladio Dieste, Church of Christ the Worker, Atlántida, Uruguay, 1960, close up of thin exterior masonry shell

FIG. 11: Dieste, Church of Christ the Worker, concave space within masonry shell

BOTTOM, LEFT TO RIGHT:

FIG. 12: Bunshaft/SOM, Beinecke Rare Book and Manuscript Library, base detail

FIG. 13: Bunshaft/SOM, Beinecke Rare Book and Manuscript Library, exterior detail

FIG. 14: Bunshaft/SOM, Beinecke Rare Book and Manuscript Library, interior showing light-transmitting marble

19

MINERAL

his Church of Christ the Worker (1960) in Atlántida, Uruguay, precisely because it was more familiar to the local farmers than stucco or stone.[3] [FIG. 10] Dieste explored the little-known structural potential of reinforced masonry in the church, transforming hand-laid brick walls into structural shells. The plan of the one-room church is elementary at ground level, but the wall contours change with altitude from rectilinear lines at the base to sinusoidal waves at the top. Composed of impossibly thin brick shells, the walls were constructed without joints to be a single undulating unit like the roof. Dieste demonstrated that a humble veneer material could exhibit the structural and geometrical sophistication of thin-shell concrete structures. [FIG. 11]

While Dieste's church explores structural lightness with brick, the Beinecke Rare Book and Manuscript Library (1963) in New Haven, Connecticut, achieves visual lightness with stone. In his design for the building, Gordon Bunshaft of SOM substituted conventional glazing with translucent stone—both to convey a sense of gravitas as well as protect the rare books held within. [FIG. 12] The facade consists of

a Vierendeel frame clad in Vermont Woodbury granite on the exterior and precast concrete on the interior; the frame holds translucent white Vermont Montclair Danby marble panels in place. [FIG. 13] During daytime the 1¼ inch (3.18 cm) thick marble panes appear stark and opaque on the exterior, while sunlight highlights the deep, richly colored veining of the stone from inside. [FIG. 14] At night the relationship is reversed, transforming the enclosure into a softly glowing lantern.

Peter Zumthor's Therme Vals project (1996) exploits the power of stone to create immersive, enduring spaces. Located in a remote village in Graubünden, Switzerland, the thermal-baths structure conjures the image of a rock quarry, and its simple, rectilinear geometries made of many thin layers of stone contrast abruptly with the landscape. [FIG. 15] Zumthor minimized the material palette to highlight the basic architectural elements of stone, water, and light in the building. The concrete structure is faced with 3 feet 3 inches (1 m) long slabs of local Valser quartzite stone. The approximately sixty thousand slabs cut in three different heights (the three

TOP, LEFT TO RIGHT:
FIG. 15: Peter Zumthor, Therme Vals, Graubünden, Switzerland, 1996
FIG. 16: Zumthor, Therme Vals, exterior detail

FIG. 17: Zumthor, Therme Vals, interior

BOTTOM, LEFT TO RIGHT:
FIG. 18: Rock of Ages quarry, Barre, Vermont

FIG. 19: A mining truck transporting large stones, Kárahnjúkar, Iceland

dimensions of each slab add up to approximately 6 inches [15 cm]) create an irregular rhythm while maintaining a regular module overall. [**FIG. 16**] Interior spaces convey a brooding atmosphere reminiscent of water-filled caverns. [**FIG. 17**] A grass-covered roof completes the impression of an excavated site, rendering the Therme Vals as a modern cairn that is as ageless as it is shrewdly contemporary.

Environmental Considerations

Mineral harvesting is an environmentally disturbing activity. Most stone is mined in open quarries, requiring removal of overburden (the material that lies above an area of economic or scientific interest in mining, most commonly the rock, soil, and ecosystem above a desired ore body) and resulting in large open pits. [**FIG. 18**] The harvesting of ceramic clays and loam also involve open-pit mining; some types of limestone, marble, and slate are harvested below ground.[4] Mining generates a large amount of debris that can clog and contaminate local waterways, and releases chemicals that can leach into groundwater. Erosion and biodiversity loss, as a result, are concerns.

Careful water-control measures that control runoff must be put in place, and any new mine excavation must have a closure plan, which ensures the reparation of the landscape after operations are completed.

Although common types of stone and ceramic clays used for building are abundant, increased urbanization and consideration for environmentally sensitive regions limit the development of new mining operations in certain locations. Loam is quite easy to obtain, since it is widespread and requires a minimal depth of excavation, which explains its role in sheltering one-third of the human population.[5]

Because of the heavy weight of earthen materials, their transport requires large amounts of energy. [**FIG. 19**] Stone can be cut at the quarry but is often further processed, or "dressed," off-site. The farther the distance the stone is required to travel to a job site, the more significant its carbon footprint is. Ceramics production—particularly alumina-oxide ceramic, used in components such as electrical insulators, water-faucet valves, and mechanical seals—also demands a large amount of embodied energy (the energy input required to make a product, bring it to

FIG. 20: Mauricio Rocha, Oaxaca School of Plastic Arts, Oaxaca, Mexico, 2008, detail of rammed earth wall

FIG. 21: Changdeokgung Palace, Seoul, South Korea, 1405, detail of wall designed to store energy from ondol (under floor) heating

FIG. 22: A carbon fiber-reinforced ceramic composite by Brembo

21

market, and dispose of it). The production of ceramics involves approximately fifty times the embodied energy of concrete.[6] However, architects often justify the energy cost because of the durability and reusability of ceramics. Stone, brick, and clay tile may be easily reused at the end of their initial lives, but care must be taken during the demolition process to remove grout or other adhesives and keep the materials intact. The materials, when ground down, can be used as fill in building and infrastructure projects.

Earthen materials exhibit high thermal mass—they can be used in buildings to offset peak daytime temperatures and reduce the severity of thermal loads—resulting in lower energy costs and increased occupant comfort.[7] [**FIG. 20**] Optimal materials for thermal-mass applications exhibit high density and high heat capacity, and are an integral component in passive-solar design. [**FIG. 21**]

Disruptive Technologies

Although stone and ceramics are some of the oldest known building materials, they remain the focus of continued research. Ceramic materials in particular have been the subject of significant technological advances in recent decades—such as the ability to achieve high strength or optical transparency. Some of these new iterations share little in common with their neolithic predecessors. In terms of mechanical performance, ceramic, stone, and the other mineral-based materials covered in this section are valued for their high compressive strength. Durability is also a key factor in their ongoing use. Emerging

technologies in this category capitalize on these positive traits while seeking various performance- and process-related enhancements.

High prioritization is given to ceramic materials by the automotive and aerospace industries, due to their excellent resistance to heat and friction and ample compressive strength. Carbon fiber–reinforced ceramic composite materials are particularly prized for their extreme damage tolerance, rigidity, and superior wear resistance. [**FIG. 22**] Because of these favorable characteristics, manufacturers are beginning to develop carbon fiber–reinforced composites for sheathing applications in buildings.

The most recent and visible development in ceramic materials for building construction is architectural terra cotta. Although originally applied in an unglazed form in the early nineteenth century, glazed terra cotta has since become a popular product for architectural rain-screen applications due to its geometric precision, lightness, and prefabricated delivery in metal frames. These traits also make terra-cotta systems an appropriate replacement for traditional masonry construction.

Because mineral-based materials involve energy-intensive fabrication processes, manufacturers have been exploring low-energy-production alternatives—such as multifunctional wallboards made by a chemical process rather than one requiring added heat or pressure. Composed of magnesium oxide, expanded perlite, and preconsumer recycled cellulose, this type of wallboard bonds exothermically (a process or reaction that releases energy, usually

FIG.24: Transparent ceramics developed by the Fraunhofer Institute

in the form of heat) when poured into a mold at room temperature and thus requires no additional heat for its manufacture. [**FIG.23**] Given the ubiquity of wallboard and floorboard products in building construction, the incorporation of exothermically fabricated materials could make notable improvements to the environmental performance of buildings. Other materials developed to bond chemically without added heat include so-called bio bricks, made of sand, urea, and bacteria. These unconventional bricks are grown using a calcite-precipitation process rather than manufactured with added heat, and possess a strength equivalent to typical kiln-fired bricks.

Although metallic glazes and other surface treatments have long offered ceramic materials with light-reflective properties, new materials harness light in other unexpected ways. Transparent corundum and alumina-oxide ceramics provide 60 to 80 percent visible light transmission and exhibit significantly higher strength and greater heat resistance than glass. [**FIG.24**] Transparent ceramics may one day be used for blast- and heat-resistant windows as well as transparent body armor. Other materials are designed to store light rather than transmit it—such as photo-luminescent aggregates that can illuminate emergency egress pathways during power outages or provide pattern enhancements in darkened conditions—demonstrating a material's capacity for multiple readings.

New computer-automated production methods enable a variety of form- and image-transfer capabilities. Digital image–fired ceramic tiles incorporate photographic imagery by treating ceramic glazes like printing inks. Another process utilizes digital images to generate bas-relief in ceramic tiles, creating a kind of photo-topographic surface that may be painted with standard industry glazes. [**FIG.25**] Stone surfaces may also be contoured using advanced methods of three-dimensional sculpting, allowing unprecedented formal manipulation and control of the most intractable of materials.

Disruptive Applications

Mineral-based materials are inextricably associated with the architecture of the past, based on their millennia-long utilization and enduring presence. They are often used in contemporary building to connote tradition, persistence, and gravity, even if they are merely surface treatments and are not load bearing. However, it is precisely earthen materials' inseparable affiliation with the past that makes them perfect candidates for disruptive applications. The more deeply entrenched the expectations are related to substance, craft, structure, and process, the greater the effect that subtle manipulations to this material code can produce.

A common disruptive approach questions the compression-dominance of earthen materials. Studio Gang's *Marble Curtain* (2003), for example, is an expansive sheet of thin stone held in suspension. [**FIG.26**] Hung from the vaulted ceiling of the National Building Museum in Washington, DC, the 18 foot (5.49 m) tall Marble Curtain consists of 620 pieces of ⅜ inch (1 cm) thick translucent stone. [**FIG.27**]

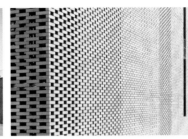

MINERAL

The stone tiles were fabricated in interlocking jigsaw puzzle–style shapes by water-jet cutting and were mounted onto a layer of fiber resin for additional structural reinforcing. Because stone has a limited history of tensile-stress testing, the fifteen-hundred-pound, light-transmitting curtain evokes surprise in its unconventional use of the material.

The opacity of traditional stone applications makes light transmission another fertile approach to disruption. Projects like Franz Füeg's St. Pius Church (1966) in Meggen, Switzerland, and Diamond and Schmitt Architects' Ministry of Foreign Affairs (2004) in Jerusalem, Israel, exhibit facades of thin, translucent stone enclosing large public spaces. In both projects this type of application takes advantage of a dual reading of the material based on the time of day, because the interior or exterior surface appears opaque while the other emits light.

Process conventions are also ripe for manipulation. Common methods used to construct masonry facades, such as hand-laid, gravity-bound surfaces, are questioned in Jun Aoki & Associates' Aomori Museum of Art (2006) in Japan, for example. [**FIG.28**] The structure is clad in sweeping monochromatic surfaces of white-painted bricks used for soffits as well as walls—a nod to the contemporary role of masonry as wallpaper. The Aomori Museum also makes extensive use of earthen floors and walls within its lower levels. Such a large-scale use of precisely packed earth in a public building is a surprising application for such a primitive and finicky material. Herzog & de Meuron's Dominus Winery (1998) in

Napa Valley, California, utilizes another unexpected material, rock-filled gabions, which are typically used to retain soil in earth-grading projects (large-scale infrastructure projects in which erosion is controlled) rather than for the construction of architectural walls.

Given their long history of use in manual-construction practices, the dimensions of bricks, tiles, and pavers are closely related to the scale of the human hand. Masonry is, therefore, often described as contributing warmth and human qualities to architecture even when it is engineered in prefabricated panels. Sunao Ando's Right-On building (2006) in Tsukuba, Japan, explores the tension between in situ hand laying and machine-driven prefabrication in its variegated brick enclosure. The precisely constructed facade exhibits seamless gradations between a closed running-bond pattern and an open weave—which allows light to infiltrate interior spaces—reminiscent of English garden-wall enclosures. [**FIG.29**]

Spanish Pavilion

Aichi
Japan Foreign Office Architects
2005

In the design of the Spanish Pavilion for the Aichi Expo in Japan, Foreign Office Architects established an architectural language signifying an integration of Western and Middle Eastern cultures. Composed of interior volumes of various sizes, the pavilion makes spatial references to Romanesque naves as well as Middle Eastern courtyard typologies.

Enveloping these spaces is a grand scrim made of tubelike ceramic tiles. The architects describe this surface as a structural lattice inspired by the use of tile in Spanish architecture. Seven geometrically varying types of hexagonal modules fabricated in six different colors create a consistent yet constantly varying pattern. The 20 inch wide x 5 inch tall (50 x 12.5 cm) ceramic elements were clipped to internal steel supports, eliminating the need for grout. The multistory ceramic screen was separated from the internal walls by a distance of 4 feet 11 inches (1.5 m), which created an interstitial space that allowed for pedestrian circulation and the filtration of light.

OPPOSITE: Exterior
TOP: Elevation showing
solid modules

BOTTOM LEFT: Ceramic scrim
BOTTOM RIGHT: Detail of
ceramic modules

25

MINERAL

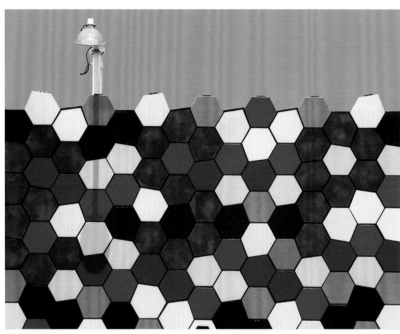

Chokkura Plaza and Shelter

Tochigi, Japan
Kengo Kuma & Associates
2006

When Frank Lloyd Wright designed the Imperial Hotel in Tokyo in 1923, he specified Oya stone for a facing material. Existing only within a 9 square miles (24 km²) area in Japan's Tochigi prefecture, Oya stone is a kind of volcanic tuff known for its resistance to fire and erosion, and for its easy workability. By the time Wright selected the stone for its rich texture, color, and softness, it had already been used in the walls and foundations of buildings in the Kanto region—of which Tochigi is a part—for centuries. In the construction boom that followed World War II, Oya-stone mining reached 900,000 tons annually until concrete became a more popular alternative construction material in the 1970s.[8]

When given the opportunity to design a building in Tochigi on the site of an abandoned rice warehouse built of Oya stone, Kengo Kuma seized the chance to work with the material. The Chokkura addition houses a community hall and exhibition gallery, and the new structure is located immediately adjacent to the existing building. Never one to use material in a conventional way, Kuma made a perforated wall using the stone, inspired by its physical porosity. In keeping with his strong aspirations to dematerialize architecture, Kuma detailed the stone wall so that the material appears to float. Alternating courses of chevron-shaped stones barely touch at their apexes and suggest impossible lightness. In reality the stones are supported by a ¼ inch (6 mm) thick steel plate—strong enough to hold the stone, yet thin enough to escape visual detection from short distances. The two materials perform structural work as a composite system: steel supports stone, and stone supports steel.

The Chokkura project embodies Kuma's search for lightness and the true expression of materials. It also exemplifies Kuma's interest in using local materials and collaborating with local craftspeople.

MINERAL

TOP: Section drawing of multipurpose exhibition hall.
BOTTOM LEFT: View from anteroom
MIDDLE RIGHT: Mock-up of wall
BOTTOM RIGHT: Construction of Oya-stone wall

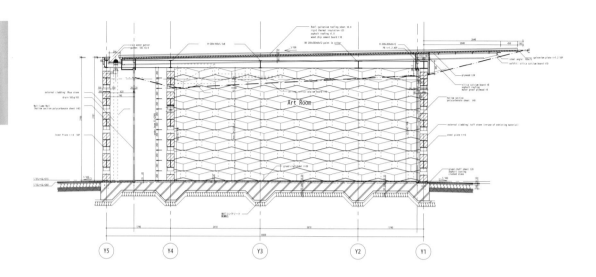

Gantenbein Winery

Fläsch, Switzerland
Gramazio & Kohler Architecture and Urbanism with Bearth & Deplazes Architekten
2006

When Bearth & Deplazes Architects hired Gramazio & Kohler to design the facade to a winery extension, the researchers at ETH Zürich only had three months to complete construction. The clients had requested a new structure to house a fermentation room for grape processing, a cellar for wine-barrel storage, and a terrace for wine tastings. Bearth & Deplazes, familiar with Gramazio & Kohler's studies in robotic fabrication, requested that the designers apply a robot-driven prefabrication method to the design and construction of the exterior infill panels of the addition.

Gramazio & Kohler created an abstract digital template based on an image of a basket filled with grapes stretched to cover the building's 4,300 square foot (400 m²) facade. They programmed a robot in their laboratory to construct panels out of individually laid bricks, and the angles at which the bricks were placed were determined by the brightness

of individual pixels of the photograph of grapes. According to the researchers, the facade projects an image with bricks just as a computer screen uses pixels—yet unlike a two-dimensional surface, its three-dimensional nature allows it to continually transform depending on the position of the viewer and the sun angle. An automated procedure regulated the application of a two-component bonding agent to the bricks, ensuring the rigidity of the panels.

The seventy-two panels making up the facade were delivered to the site on a truck and lifted into place by crane. The shifting orientations of twenty thousand bricks allow light to penetrate the structure at varying angles and intensities. The brick naturally tempers peak outdoor temperatures, and clear polycarbonate panels located on the interior block wind and rain penetration.

OPPOSITE: Facade detail
TOP: Interior-panel detail

MIDDLE: Panel detail
BOTTOM LEFT: Crane-assisted panel delivery

BOTTOM MIDDLE: On-site placement of panels
BOTTOM RIGHT: South facade

31

MINERAL

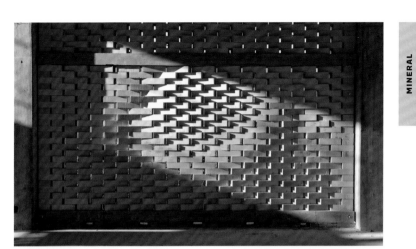

Horten

Copenhagen, Denmark
3XN
2009

New energy standards and more stringent environmental codes have added complexity to the already challenging process of designing buildings. Not only does Horten law firm's new office building require less energy than stipulated by Danish code, but it also delivers the seemingly impossible: a corner office for every employee. Architecture firm 3XN approached the project with the goal to prove that high-performance buildings can also be formally provocative.

The firm exploited the facade for the purposes of passive-solar design. By angling vertical strip windows on the east and west facades to face the Copenhagen waterfront to the north, the architects significantly reduced the amount of solar heat gain on the glazing and lowered the building's energy load by 10 percent. This strategy also resulted in a highly animated, multidimensional envelope made of staggered bands of faceted planes. Redefining the conventional stone-clad corporate office, 3XN devised an insulated composite panel faced with travertine that could be easily integrated within a complex curtain-wall system. The panel consists of an insulating-foam core sandwiched between two layers of fiberglass sheeting; a layer of stone placed on the exterior side of the panel expresses the visual grain and texture of stone within a lightweight, thermally optimized panel. Although the design represents a departure from traditional stone facades, it retains the spirit of the material—conjuring images of jagged cliffs drenched in sunlight.

OPPOSITE: View of faceted stone and glass planes
TOP: View of building entrance

MIDDLE: West facade
BOTTOM LEFT: Panel made of travertine on fiberglass sheeting with insulating-foam core

BOTTOM RIGHT: Panel mock-up

33

MINERAL

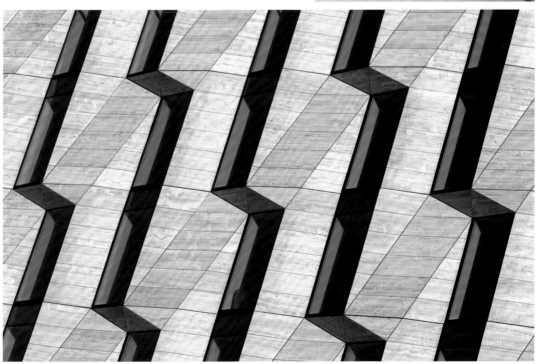

Ningbo Historical Museum

Ningbo, China
Amateur Architecture Studio
2009

The condition of the palimpsest is evident throughout architectural history. The life of a building and its materials is not a fixed condition but rather a continually evolving enterprise. The Romans pilfered construction materials from older edifices to build new monuments, and medieval populations later pillaged Roman monuments for their building blocks. Given the profound material changes that architecture experiences over time, futurist Steward Brand, in *How Buildings Learn: What Happens After They're Built* (1995), suggests that we define architecture not as "the art of building," but rather as "the design-science of the life of buildings."

The Chinese practice of *wapan* tiling evolved as a method for building walls rapidly using available materials in a region subject to frequent typhoons. Amateur Architecture Studio chose this cladding method for its design of the Ningbo Historical

Museum, reusing the various types of bricks and tiles that remained after the city government razed dozens of villages to make way for a new central business district. Principal Wang Shu led local masons in constructing the walls, allowing them to have a large degree of freedom in laying the dissimilar blocks. The rich detail provided by the hand-laid tiles complements the hulking mass of the museum, and the randomly placed, various-sized apertures embrace the spirit of the wapan approach.

In today's rapidly developing China, the image of brick-and-tile rubble left over from recently demolished structures is unfortunately an all-too-common sight. The walls of the Ningbo Historical Museum thus serve as a haunting reminder of the past, encapsulating the bones of vanished villages in a monument that pays its respects to history at the same time it has come to supersede it.

38　**TOP:** Concrete cast with bamboo
formwork and wapan tiling
MIDDLE: Detail of wapan tiling
BOTTOM: Roof terrace

CONCRETE

CONCRETE

There is also a kind of powder which from natural causes produces astonishing results....This substance, when mixed with lime and rubble, not only lends strength to buildings of other kinds, but even when piers of it are constructed in the sea, they set hard under water. – Vitruvius

Concrete is a product of the impulse to replicate the beauty and permanence of stone with the pliancy of a viscous liquid during the casting stage. It is considered the first artificial, as well as hybrid, material and has played a pivotal role in the history of building construction given its widespread use.[1] Concrete exhibits the characteristic of *simplexity*—it is a material simple enough to be mass-produced and widely adopted yet complex in its composition and difficult to perfect. Concrete now is so broadly used—at an annual rate of five billion cubic yards—that it ranks second only to water as the most consumed substance in the world.[2]

According to technology historian Antoine Picon, "no material has been more closely associated with the origins and development of modern architecture than concrete."[3] With its ease of use and ubiquity throughout the constructed environment, concrete has come to embody both the agency and anonymity of the modern condition. On one hand, concrete represents the pinnacle of technological achievement, demonstrated by SOM's Burj Khalifa (2010) in Dubai, United Arab Emirates, the tallest building in the world (see page 48, figure 22); on the other hand, concrete is symbolic of the alienating and antiseptic aspects of modern construction and development, represented by the omnipresence of drab, impervious structures in heavily urbanized areas.

Because concrete can be used in a variety of ways and assumes many different forms—unlike the more specific and predictable character of brick and steel—architects struggle with defining the true nature of concrete, which Frank Lloyd Wright called a "mongrel" material due to its ambiguous character.[4] Concrete has enabled the realization of unprecedented plasticity in modern architecture— yet its name suggests something solid and definitive. [FIGS. 1+2] Tadao Ando envisions that concrete can approach the beauty of Portland stone (after which the modern variant of cement, portland cement, was named). [FIGS. 3+4] Other approaches include the search for new and unique manifestations of the material.

Composition

Concrete is made of aggregates of different sizes and a cement binder that is activated by water. Cement consists of limestone, silicon, calcium, and often aluminum and iron, and is offered in multiple types, including Type I (general use), II (moderate heat of hydration), III (high early strength), IV (low heat of hydration), and V (sulfate resistant). The composition of concrete is typically six parts water, four parts coarse aggregate (gravel), two parts fine aggregate (sand), and one part portland cement. Originally developed by British mason Joseph Aspdin in 1824, portland cement is the accepted international standard cement. It is made by grinding a combination of limestone and clay, and sintering it to 1400 to 1450°C in order to create alite and belite, which are minerals that form calcium silicate hydrate and calcium hydroxide and provide concrete its strength.

Because concrete behaves poorly when subjected to tensile stresses, it is nearly always reinforced. Steel bars, mesh, and wire, or a combination of the three, are strategically placed prior to casting to provide adequate tensile strength. Concrete and steel

TOP, LEFT TO RIGHT:
FIG.1: Antoni Gaudí, Sagrada Familia, Barcelona, Spain, 1882– , interior detail
FIG.2: Louis Kahn, Salk Institute for Biological Studies, La Jolla, California, 1963

FIG.3: Tadao Ando, Hyogo Prefectural Museum of Art, Kobe, Japan, 2002
FIG.4: Tadao Ando Architects & Associates, Church on the Water, Tomamu, Japan, 1988, interior-wall detail

BOTTOM, LEFT TO RIGHT:
FIG.5: Basilica of Maxentius, Rome, Italy, 312 CE, detail of coffered concrete vault with brick cladding
FIG.6: Pantheon, Rome, Italy, 118 CE, detail of oculus

43

CONCRETE

also make a good marriage in that they have similar coefficients of thermal expansion (the amount that a material will expand with each degree of temperature increase), and concrete protects steel from fire as well as rust. Concrete makes use of various admixtures, such as accelerators, shrinkage reducers, or superplasticizers, and may incorporate supplementary cementitious materials, like blast-furnace slag or fly ash, as partial cement replacements.

Concrete is created by an exothermic reaction that results from cement hydration—which hardens and increases the strength of concrete—and generally requires twenty-eight days to reach optimal compressive strength. In the construction industry, a distinction is made based on concrete's casting location—either in position on-site (cast-in-place) or off-site (precast).

History

Archaeological records reveal the use of lime-based mortar as early as 12,000 BCE, and Egyptian builders employed concrete in the construction of the pyramids.[5] The Romans developed this material further into what they called *opus caementicium*, a combination of pumice aggregate, quicklime, and pozzolana (volcanic ash). Roman builders cast this material in layers with hand-laid rubble and typically clad it with another material, such as stone or kiln-fired bricks. [**FIG.5**] Concrete played a significant part in establishing the technological legacy of Roman building, as it enabled the expedient construction of arches, vaults, and domes without the difficulties presented by masonry. Completed in 118 CE, the Roman Pantheon possesses a concrete rotunda with an impressive span of 144 feet (44m)—the largest single building span until the nineteenth century, more than seventeen hundred years later.[6] [**FIG.6**]

The history of concrete reveals the disjointed trajectory of the development of technology. Despite the great feats of engineering accomplished with concrete, the application of opus caementicium largely disappeared with the fall of Rome—although historians point to a few medieval uses of concrete in Europe, indicating its continuous, if infrequent, use. After a span of thirteen centuries, three important discoveries enabled the production of modern concrete. In 1756

FIG. 7: Le Corbusier, Notre Dame du Haut, Ronchamp, France, 1955

FIG. 8: Le Corbusier, Notre Dame du Haut, exterior view showing exposed concrete roof and gunite walls

FIG. 9: Le Corbusier, Notre Dame du Haut, interior with light-transmitting slot visible near the ceiling

the engineer John Smeaton developed a concrete mix using pebbles with hydraulic lime, which cured in the presence of water. In 1824 Aspdin developed portland cement, named after the highly prized limestone quarried on the Isle of Portland in Dorset, United Kingdom. Two decades later inventor Joseph-Louis Lambot created ferro-cement, or what we refer to as reinforced concrete, by incorporating iron bars within cast concrete to resist tensile stresses in water tanks and boats. Engineers became fascinated with the idea of making ferro-cement buildings, and in 1893 the erection of the California-based Pacific Coast Borax Company refinery by Ernest L. Ransome heralded the first reinforced-concrete building in the United States.

Modern Precedents

By the dawn of the twentieth century, the Age of Concrete had begun. Initially used in the construction of industrial warehouses and factories, reinforced concrete was soon used to accommodate other building programs. Auguste Perret used the material for the facade of an apartment block in Paris in 1903. His disciple Le Corbusier demonstrated the newfound freedoms permitted by reinforced-concrete technology in his Domino System of 1914—a prototypical structural framework that eliminated the load-bearing requirement of the facade—establishing the conceptual significance of this technological approach.

Although concrete became the basis for a new iteration of the trabeated form of construction characterized by linear beams, columns, and plates, and typically of masonry and wood, Le Corbusier's Notre

Dame du Haut (1955) signified a departure from this rational system. [**FIGS. 7+8**] Located in Ronchamp, France, the highly sculptural chapel is a reinforced-concrete structure with masonry infill and a 1½ inch (4 cm) coating of gunite, a spray-applied concrete. A heavy roof of rough, exposed concrete, or *béton brut*, forms a stark contrast against the white-washed surfaces of the walls. The architect intentionally thickened the building enclosure for dramatic effect. What initially appear to be massive bearing walls do not actually support the structure—a fact revealed by a 4 inch (10 cm) tall horizontal slot running between the top of the walls and the roof, within which one can see the profiles of relatively thin concrete columns. [**FIG. 9**]

The treatment of concrete as a plastic material capable of blurring structure and skin at Ronchamp inspired many subsequent designs. Meanwhile, another trajectory utilized concrete as a refined substance capable of expressing the optimization of structural-loading patterns. Louis Kahn's Kimbell Art Museum is a celebrated example of this approach. [**FIG. 10**] Constructed in Fort Worth, Texas, in 1972, the 120,000 square foot (11,148 m²) museum is composed of a modular array of linear galleries and three interstitial garden courts. Its reinforced-concrete frame is at once highly rational and surprising: exposed concrete columns mark the rectangular corners of the galleries, but the relatively slender 2 x 2 foot (61 x 61 cm) columns impossibly support 100 foot (30.48 m) spans. Furthermore, what appear to be barrel-vault roofs are contradicted by the startling

insertion of a 30 inch (76.2 cm) linear space along each vault's apex for the admission of light. [FIG.11] Each half-vault is, in reality, a cycloid shell of post-tensioned reinforced concrete—an architectural feature that represents not only an ingenious structural solution but also an elegant surface for the diffusion of sunlight.

In the era following Kahn's death, the work of Ando represents the pinnacle of fair-face-concrete architecture.[7] Developed during the early stage of his career in works like his 1976 Row House in Sumiyoshi, Ando's perfected version of fair-faced concrete is perhaps most celebrated in his canonical Church of the Light (1989) in Ibaraki, Osaka, Japan. [FIGS.12+13] The intimate, 1,200 square foot (113 m^2) chapel is a single space defined by a simple rectilinear enclosure of reinforced concrete penetrated by a wall angled at 15 degrees that encloses an exterior garden. The uncannily smooth concrete surface bears Ando's signature use of panel-spaced control joints and perfectly aligned form ties, indicating a construction process of the highest levels of rigor. The spartan volume is penetrated on one side by two perpendicular apertures that form a cross—an interpretation of the crucifix as a void. Like Ronchamp and the Kimbell, this void induces surprise since the upper quadrants of the wall appear to be unsupported from the inside, and the building triggers dual readings of gravitas and weightlessness.

Environmental Considerations

From a standpoint as a physical resource, concrete is a very accommodating material. Its primary ingredients—gravel, sand, and water—may be found virtually anywhere, and cement is relatively easy to obtain. The fact that the mix can be tailored with various aggregates and supplementary cementitious materials enhances its appeal. Where concrete presents an environmental challenge is in the large amount of energy required to produce cement clinker (a hydraulic material ground with chemical admixtures to produce cement). [FIG.14]

Although cement makes up only 12 percent of the total weight of concrete, it is responsible for 94 percent of its embodied energy—roughly 3 MJ/kg. Because of the large quantity of concrete produced, the material is responsible for approximately 6 to 8 percent of the global carbon footprint—producing one ton of portland cement contributes about one ton of carbon dioxide to the atmosphere. However, recent kiln technologies have reduced the energy requirement of cement production by half, and future cement kilns may be able to minimize energy levels to rates as low as 2 MJ/kg. On-site batching plants minimize the energy required for the transportation of concrete, and the use of high-performance concrete can reduce the total volume of required material for a building.

Concrete casting demands a large amount of water, which typically has to be potable since impurities can cause efflorescence and staining in the material. Salt-water concrete is currently under development and would allow the use of seawater for coastal construction. High volume fly ash (HVFA)

  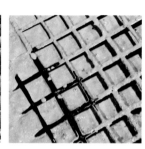

concrete uses the fly ash by-product of coal production to offset a large percentage of the cement needed for concrete production. HVFA concrete not only redirects material from the waste stream but also has a lower embodied energy than traditional concrete. Similar to the pozzolanic volcanic ash harvested by Roman builders to make opus caementitium, industrial fly ash consists of 60 to 90 percent fine silica beads that allow for good compaction and result in a more durable concrete than when using conventional cement. [**FIG.15**] Although fly ash contains trace amounts of lead, mercury, and dioxins, these substances are more likely to leach out of landfills than cast concrete. HVFA concrete typically requires longer setting times and must be handled more carefully than regular concrete to ensure consistent strength.

Concrete is technically recyclable, although it is most often downcycled for roadwork and other low-grade construction. Concrete from demolished structures can be crushed and reused as large aggregate in new mixes. However, this type of application requires more cement than would be necessary when using only new material, increasing the carbon footprint and negating the benefits of using recycled aggregate.

When used in the building envelope, concrete helps fulfill a passive-solar strategy because of its high thermal mass. This property allows concrete to absorb, store, and later release large amounts of heat—the result is delayed and reduced peak energy loads in buildings. This thermal-mass effect operates in a range of climates and is most successful when the concrete is exposed on the interior of the building.

Insulating concrete forms (ICF) offer another means of achieving an energy reduction. Consisting of insulation-based formwork modules that remain after the concrete is cast, ICF exhibit high thermal resistance with R-values typically in excess of R-17. (R-value is a common measure of thermal resistance used by the building-construction industry—the higher the value, the greater the insulating efficacy.)

Disruptive Technologies

Reinforced concrete represents a technological paradox. On one hand, its ubiquity as the utilitarian substance of modern construction makes concrete the most common, predictable, and seemingly unsophisticated of materials. On the other hand, concrete has become the subject of intense research scrutiny—in part due to its omnipresence—and concrete technology has become profoundly varied and complex, often generating surprising results. The disruptive technologies featured here acknowledge concrete's pervasiveness and push its utilization efficiency as well as its aesthetic potential.

Because of the large carbon footprint of concrete production, there is a concerted effort for new technologies that use resources more efficiently. Carbon-fiber-reinforced concrete replaces conventional steel with carbon-fiber reinforcing, resulting in a 66 percent weight reduction when compared with steel-reinforced concrete and decreasing transportation costs as well as the carbon footprint. [**FIG.16**]

FIG. 17: FibreC high-performance concrete, Rieder Faserbeton-Elemente GmbH

FIG. 18: Engineered Cement Composites, also known as bendable concrete, developed at the University of Michigan

FIG. 19: TX Active photocatalytic concrete by Italcementi reduces local air pollution in sunlight.

47

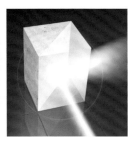

Ultra-high-performance concretes (UHPC) similarly maximize the strength-to-weight ratio of material with the incorporation of silica fume, superplasticizers, ground quartz, and mineral fibers to create materials with high strength and ductility, as well as superior resistance to impact, corrosion, and abrasion. High compressive and flexural strengths, in particular, permit the use of longer spans with thinner structural sections. Some high-performance concretes include layers of fiberglass bundles oriented in different directions to eliminate the need for steel reinforcing altogether, resulting in lightweight, highly resilient materials with superior fire resistance. [**FIG. 17**] One surprising variation of high-performance concrete is actually designed to bend under stress. With reinforcing fibers that slide independently from the aggregate and cement, the so-called engineered cement composites (ECC) can self-heal by filling microfissures with calcium carbonate in the presence of water and carbon dioxide, promising a longer lifespan than that of conventional concrete. [**FIG. 18**]

Because of the pervasiveness of the use of concrete, scientists are keen on improving the material's functionality, particularly in terms of environmental ramifications. One goal is environmental remediation, which concerns processes by which a material can improve the physical conditions of its context (the reduction of air pollution by photocatalysis is an example). Photocatalytic concrete reduces the amount of local air pollution with assistance from sunlight. [**FIG. 19**] Titanium dioxide in the concrete's hydraulic binder causes harmful particles, such as

nitrogen oxides and volatile organic compounds, to decompose into benign ones in the presence of sunlight, improving air quality. This concrete also has the capacity to self-clean, and organic substances, such as dirt, oil, and grime, break down rather than stain the surface of the material. Another remediating material is carbon-dioxide-absorbing concrete, which contains high levels of magnesium oxide and absorbs a large amount of carbon dioxide from the atmosphere as it cures.

As a mixture of multiple ingredients, concrete has inspired countless improvisations on its basic recipe. One variation has been the addition or substitution of ingredients with waste materials—as long as the performance of the concrete can be maintained, such a modification diverts resources from the waste stream and reduces the amount of new material used. About 125 million tons of coal-combustion by-products are produced in the United States annually, and the Environmental Protection Agency has set a target of a 50 percent reuse rate for these by-products in commercial applications.[8] Mentioned previously, waste-repurposing concretes make use of fly ash, silica fume, and slag from coal production—materials that can replace up to 80 percent of conventional cement, which accounts for up to 8 percent of annual global carbon-dioxide emissions.[9]

Another reuse application involves waste glass, which accounts for over seven million tons of material sent to landfills in the United States annually.[10] Precast concrete incorporating waste glass can consist of as much as 75 percent postconsumer and

FIG. 20: Eco X fiber-reinforced recycled-glass concrete by Meld USA

FIG. 21: Pixa concrete video screen by SensiTile Systems

FIG. 22: SOM, Burj Khalifa, Dubai, United Arab Emirates, 2010

FIG. 23: Alvaro Siza Vieira, Portugal Pavilion, Lisbon, Portugal, 1998

postindustrial glass that has been diverted from landfills. [**FIG. 20**]

Since the beginning of the twenty-first century, inventors in different parts of the globe have focused on achieving the same goal independently: translucent concrete. Although each approach is unique, all of them incorporate polymer strands into precast-concrete blocks or slabs to propagate light through concrete's opaque mass. One version utilizes thousands of embedded, parallel fiber-optic strands; another makes use of solid, transparent plastic rods; and yet another employs translucent fabric. Each technology allows light and shadow to travel through walls many feet thick, defying the assumption that concrete is necessarily opaque. The placement of light-transmitting materials at regular intervals in concrete, in conjunction with LED lighting, allows for the fabrication of concrete video screens. [**FIG. 21**]

New methods of digital production have influenced both the fabrication and surface manipulation of concrete. A process called contour crafting enables the three-dimensional printing of concrete for building construction. The digitally controlled procedure employs a large gantry crane with a robotic armature to deposit multiple layers of material on a site to create large-scale constructions. Digital tools have also increased the level of control and the possible variety of geometrical manipulations achievable in concrete formwork, such as the transfer of high-resolution-photographic images or intricate embossed patterns to concrete surfaces.

Disruptive Applications

Concrete continues to demonstrate significant potential in structural as well as surfacing applications. Once limited to low-slung structures or buildings with shorter spans, concrete has demonstrated unprecedented capacity in achieving a record-setting altitude. Completed in 2010, the Burj Khalifa is the world's tallest building at 2,717 feet (828 m), greatly surpassing the next tallest structure—the steel Taipei 101 (C. Y. Lee & Partners, 2004)—by more than 1,000 feet (300 m). [**FIG. 22**] Made possible by new high-strength-concrete technologies, this milestone marks the first time that the world's tallest tower has been made of concrete, for the history of the skyscraper has been largely a study of the development of the steel frame.[11] Advances in high-performance concrete and innovative casting methods continue to open new territories for the material.

Another unexpected development is the exploration of tensile properties in concrete. The Portugal Pavilion (1998) designed by Alvaro Siza Vieira exhibits a thin, curved concrete-shell roof supported at each end by steel cables. [**FIG. 23**] This daring fabrication of a long-spanning concrete-roof slab slung between two supports evokes experiments in ductile concrete designed to bend under stress.

In addition to increased performance, architects are also pursuing the integration of structure and skin in the construction of complex concrete shells. Steven Holl's Simmons Hall dormitory at MIT (2002) was inspired by the internal geometry of a sponge, and the so-called perfcon (perforated concrete) model was

FIG. 24: Steve Holl Architects, Simmons Hall at MIT, Cambridge, Massachusetts, 2002

FIG. 25: Tadao Ando Architect & Associates, Himeji City Museum of Literature, Hyogo, Japan, 1991-96, interior detail.

FIG. 26: Giampaolo Imbrighi, City of Man Pavilion, Shanghai, China, 2010, detail of i.light light-transmitting-concrete panel

FIG. 27: VJAA, Monastery Guesthouse at St. John's Abbey, Collegeville, Minnesota, 2008, detail of light-emitting concrete blocks

49

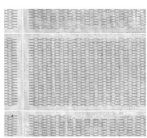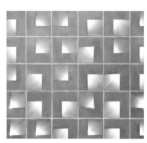

intended to provide maximum programmatic flexibility as well as possibilities for enhanced interaction. [**FIG. 24**] Zaha Hadid envisioned the Phaeno Science Center (2005) in Wolfsburg, Germany, as a series of concrete cones elevated above an urban landscape. The cones not only support the building, which is free of conventional point-support columns, but also structure the spatial sequence of the museum.

Ando's masterful use of exposed concrete continues to inspire the pursuit of perfection in finish quality. [**FIG. 25**] Vaillo + Irigaray's Joyería D project (2007) in Pamplona, Spain, uses layers of ultrathin, precision-finished precast-concrete panels to create a gently undulating space. Trahan Architects' Holy Rosary Church Complex (2004) outside Baton Rouge, Louisiana, exhibits a superior level of refinement with its bright, light-reflecting concrete. The increased use of white concrete has also been influenced by the development of photocatalyzing cement, which reduces local pollution. Richard Meier's Jubilee Church (2003) in Rome, for example, is composed of a series of large fin-shaped structures clad in white concrete containing high levels of titanium dioxide, which has been proven to reduce local levels of nitrogen dioxide.

The ability of concrete to transmit light continues to fascinate architects, and translucent concrete is being applied at more expansive scales. Giampaolo Imbrighi's design for the City of Man Pavilion (2010) in Shanghai employs light-emitting-concrete panels made of i.light transparent cement. The 39 x 20 x 2 inch (100 x 50 x 5 cm) panels consist of a plastic-resin matrix that allows for up to 20 percent light transmittance. [**FIG. 26**] Covering 40 percent of the pavilion exterior, the panels appear solid from the light-directed side but translucent from behind. Light transmission can be a compelling pursuit even when the material itself is opaque. VJAA's facade for the Monastery Guesthouse at St. John's Abbey (2008) in Collegeville, Minnesota, for example, features custom-profile concrete-masonry units that conduct light via acute angles within the blocks, enlivening the wall surface with many small, indirect apertures. [**FIG. 27**]

CONCRETE

Bruder Klaus Chapel

Mechernich, Germany
Peter Zumthor
2007

Standing alone in an empty field, Peter Zumthor's Bruder Klaus Chapel initially appears as a monolith disconnected from its surroundings. A gravel path leads to a single triangular opening marked by a large steel panel, which is occasionally crossed by visitors and architectural pilgrims. Inside, the monument is a dark, womblike space, with a conical void that rises vertically to meet a teardrop-shaped opening in the roof. The walls bear a ribbed texture and ashen color, and are perforated with tiny apertures.

Commissioned by a farming couple, Herman-Josef and Trudel Scheidtweiler, the chapel honors the Swiss Saint Niklaus von Flüe—or Brother Klaus—who during his final days became a hermit and lived in a ravine. Zumthor's "architectural crevasse" was made by first constructing a tepee form, using 112 slender trees obtained from a local forest, on a concrete platform. The entire structure was then enveloped in concrete, which was poured in 20 inch (50 cm) tall layers that were each compressed by hand using wood forms. Zumthor called the mixture of river gravel, orange sand, and white cement "rammed concrete," in part because of its resemblance to rammed earth. One casting was made per day for twenty-four days, resulting in a 39 foot (12 m) tall tower.

The architect then ignited the interior timbers, which burned for three weeks. The fire left behind a charred, blackened surface with scalloped ridges where the trees once stood. The holes remaining from the presence of the concrete-form ties were plugged with mouth-blown glass, adding a shimmering effect to the walls. A local artisan treated the floor by successively ladling molten batches of recycled lead-tin alloy on top of the concrete foundation, creating a mottled surface that scatters and diffuses the intense light entering the oculus above.

OPPOSITE: Exterior view
TOP: The monolithic chapel
in context

MIDDLE LEFT: Interior view
of oculus
MIDDLE RIGHT: Entrance

BOTTOM LEFT: Corner detail
BOTTOM RIGHT: Detail of rammed
concrete wall showing form-
tie holes

51

CONCRETE

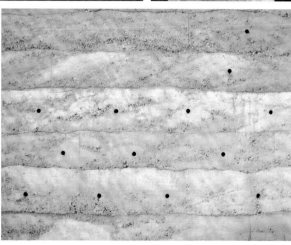

Cella Septichora Visitor Center

Pécs, Hungary
Bachman & Bachmann Architects
2007

Concrete has deeply embedded connotations of solidity and gravitas; the English word *concrete* means something "solid," "real," and "definitive." Developed by Hungarian architect and inventor Áron Losonczi, Light Transmitting Concrete (Litracon) startled the world with its unveiling at the National Building Museum's Liquid Stone exhibition in 2004. Prior to 2001, light transmission in concrete was a hypothetical aspiration. The incorporation of 4 percent optical fibers running parallel with the thickness of the precast modules allows for crisp renditions of light and shadow without sacrificing the structural strength of concrete.

For the design of the Cella Septichora Visitor Center, Bachman & Bachmann Architects applied Losonczi's disruptive technology as an integral part of the entry sequence. Setting 4 inch (10 cm) thick blocks of Litracon within a large steel frame, the architects created a solid concrete wall that also functions as a door—a two-ton hinged panel that swings open to accommodate heavy crowds during peak visiting hours. The use of Litracon is symbolic of the building's function in preserving a UNESCO World Heritage designated site: Just as archaeologists uncovered the early Christian burial complex below deep layers of sediment, the architects use Litracon to hint at what is on the other side of the wall through the thickness of solid concrete. By day, shadows of unwitting pedestrians are revealed to building occupants; by night, the architecture is illuminated from within, disclosing its contents.

OPPOSITE: Interior detail
showing shadows cast from
the exterior

TOP LEFT: Wall mock-up
MIDDLE LEFT: Litracube light
prototype

TOP RIGHT: The entrance to
the visitor center
BOTTOM: Interior

53

CONCRETE

RATP Bus Center

Thiais, France
ECDM Architects
2007

Surfaces impervious to moisture permeate urban environments. In commercial and industrial contexts, the area covered by concrete, asphalt, or building rooftops is often more than two-thirds. Oppressive low albedo (heat storing and dissipating) contexts can make for undesirable building sites, but ECDM Architects decided to embrace the spirit of the gritty, industrial landscape south of Paris in their design for a transit hub. As the nexus for bus lines going to and from the south and east of Paris, the RATP Bus Center serves three hundred buses and eight hundred bus drivers daily. Situated within a uniform material territory, the building is a large, slablike extrusion of the groundscape, strategically perforated with glassy voids for access and light.

From afar the building appears to be clad in the same concrete that covers its site. However, its facade is actually composed of a much more refined material, Ductal high-performance concrete, which exhibits superior ductility, durability, and lightness when compared with conventional concrete. The concrete was precast in fiber-reinforced panels only 1³⁄₁₆ inches (3 cm) thick. In demonstration of Ductal's super-plasticity, the architects designed the formwork to articulate an embossed dot pattern on the material's surface—uncannily precise for concrete. Creating a surface reminiscent of LEGO blocks and a mere ¼ inch (7 mm) tall and 1 inch (24 mm) in diameter, the dots add texture and aesthetic variation to the otherwise monochromatic facade.

The architects also used the concrete panels for the horizontal paved surface adjacent to the building, creating an exaggerated cove base where the modules join the vertical wall panels—as if the ground were being lifted in a dramatic upsurge. The curved parapet reinforces the appearance of surface continuity, conveying the architects' idea that the building lacks a clear beginning and end.

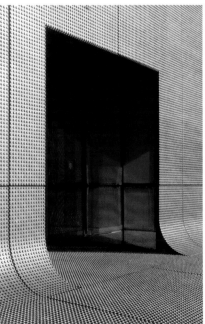

Zaragoza Bridge Pavilion

Zaragoza, Spain
Zaha Hadid Architects
2008

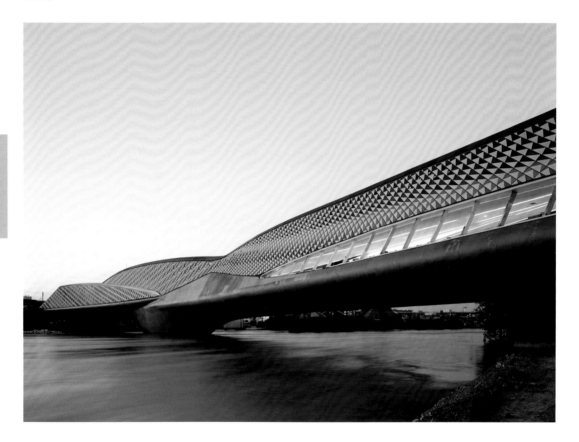

The streamlined, gently curved form of Zaha Hadid's covered bridge in Zaragoza has less in common with conventional bridges than with the high-speed racing boats that pass underneath it. The 69,050 square foot (6,415 m²) structure was designed as a multilevel entrance pavilion to the 2008 Zaragoza Expo, accommodating pedestrian traffic across the Ebro River and providing space for exhibitions. The 886 foot (270 m) long, 98 foot (30 m) tall bridge consists of two sections joined by a vertical support that straddles a small island below. Three triangular steel tube trusses at one end intersect with one truss of the other side, with hexagonal box beams acting as the top chord and steel-plate pedestrian walkways serving as the bottom chord.

The trusses are clad in panels made of FibreC high-performance concrete. Made of sand, cement, and 10 percent glass fibers, the panels are formed in structural layers with bundles of the fibers in the middle, thus requiring no steel reinforcing. The absence of steel enables the fabrication of extremely thin panels that can accommodate more complex geometrical forms than conventional steel-reinforced concrete. Twenty-nine thousand triangular panels with precisely defined spatial nodes make up the skin of the pavilion. The intricate assembly is suggestive of complex, multiscalar membranes, like the skin of fish or snakes, which are smooth surfaces formed by aggregations of small, angular modules.

OPPOSITE: Close up of bridge
midsection

TOP: Detail of high-
performance-concrete panels
BOTTON: Close up of bridge
midsection

57

CONCRETE

0-14 Tower, Dubai

United Arab Emirates
Reiser + Umemoto
2010

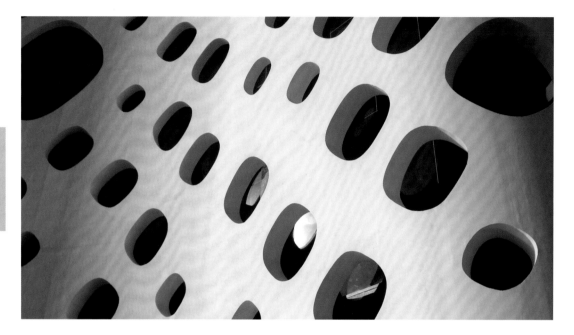

During the last two decades, the design of tall buildings has relied increasingly on the diagrid, a diamond-shaped-lattice structure that enhances rigidity while offering various possibilities for the integration of structure and skin. While diagrids have been most heavily utilized in steel construction, advances in concrete technology coupled with increasingly sophisticated structural-engineering software programs have enabled the adoption of the approach in reinforced-concrete construction. Concrete applications tend to express greater design freedom than those of steel, often blurring visible distinctions between structure and surface.

Jesse Reiser and Nanako Umemoto's 0-14 Tower is an example of the free interpretation of the diagrid in concrete. The 0-14 is a twenty-one story, 340,000 square foot (31,400 m²) office tower located along a prominent waterfront esplanade in Dubai. The tower has a porous concrete shell that is pinched at the midpoints of the sides of a rectangular plan, enhancing the reading of the building as a self-supporting tube.

The 0-14 eschews the conventional curtain-wall model and instead provides a multilayered facade—concrete exterior with a interior layer of glass—in which the outer concrete shell acts as a solar-shading device as well as a 3 foot 3 inch (1 m) deep displacement ventilation shaft.

The architects placed approximately thirteen hundred openings of various sizes within the concrete shell based on structural requirements as well as the minimization of direct solar exposure and the provision of views. These openings were constructed by inserting computer-numerical-controlled (CNC) polystyrene void forms within densely packed bundles of reinforcing steel prior to the casting of the high-strength self-consolidating concrete. The resulting biomorphic structural membrane is a tower facade absent of the expected horizontal floor lines and the vertical-column and window-mullion lines, subverting conventional readings of scale and program while also enhancing the building's environmental performance.

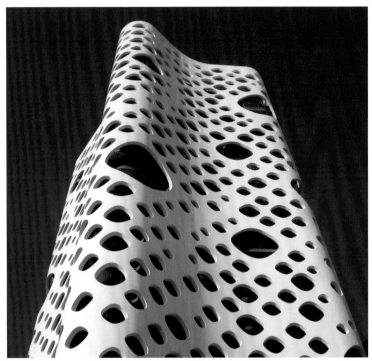

CONCRETE

WOOD

WOOD

The flows of energy and mineral nutrients through an ecosystem manifest themselves as actual animals and plants of a particular species. — Ian G. Simmons

Wood has been used in construction since before written history and is one of the most familiar and tacitly appreciated materials. Because it is a living substance until it is harvested, wood is a material that imparts an intimate haptic warmth—its tissue echoing the cellular structure of human skin. Wood is associated with strength, lightness, warmth, and tactility, and is subject to decay like any natural material. It also aids in both creation and destruction: it may be used to build or burned for heat. According to architect Luis Fernández-Galiano, "the primitive hut and the primitive fire are revealed to be inseparable," and this coupling defines "the singular and unrepeatable moment, in which architecture is born in myth, in rite, or in consciousness."[1]

Stone and wood are associated with the original forms of shelter. While stone represents a discovered place (cave), wood indicates a fabricated space (nest). [FIG.1] Wood is inseparable from the image of the primitive hut. [FIG.2] As architect Paolo Portoghesi states, "In ancient China, the ideograms that designated the concepts of 'tree' and of 'house' were so similar that they could be easily misinterpreted. The tree was the home of the primitive man and its cut trunk suggested the noble archetypal idea of the column."[2] [FIG.3] Indeed, stone columns and their acanthus leaf capitals are abstract embodiments of trees from which preneolithic structures were built—engineered groves or the architectural transubstantiation of the primeval forest.

Composition

Wood originates from matter and energy that are converted into living biomass. It is a fibrous material made of xylem, the vascular plant tissue that propagates nutrients and water and provides structural support. [FIG.4] Xylem consist of rigid, elongated cells oriented in the direction of fluid movement. The cell walls are 40 to 50 percent cellulose, 20 to 30 percent hemicellulose, 20 to 30 percent lignin, and up to 10 percent extractives. Cellulose provides tensile strength and is the most prolific natural material on earth; hemicellulose provides compressive strength and acts as a filler substance; and lignin is relatively inflexible and contributes to the rigidity of cells.

Wood is a high-strength-to-ratio material that exhibits anisotropy, which means that it has different properties along different axes. It is also hygroscopic, able to absorb or adsorb water molecules from its local environment. Wood has a low thermal conductivity and is a repository for carbon, which a tree stores throughout its lifetime in its transformation of carbon dioxide to oxygen.

The more than thirty thousand wood species exhibit significant variety in characteristics, and approximately five hundred of those are commonly used in industry.[3] Wood species are separated into softwood and hardwood classifications. Softwoods come from evergreen trees and have a simpler structure of the two classes; hardwoods derive from deciduous and broadleaf trees, and exhibit greater complexity in their composition. In building construction, softwoods are generally used for structural framing and sheathing, while hardwoods are applied in millwork and finishes.

History

Because many primitive humans lived in or near forests, they gained extensive experience using wood as a building material. Despite this established history, early wood construction remains shrouded in mystery because of its ephemerality—wood's tendency

TOP, LEFT TO RIGHT:
FIG. 1: Patrick Dougherty, *Call of the Wild* at the Museum of Glass, Tacoma, Washington, 2002, oculus framed with twigs and saplings

FIG. 2: Genka-sen well, Kinkakuji, Kyoto, Japan, early fifteenth century
FIG. 3: Wooden pavilion at the Summer Palace, Beijing, China, 1750

BOTTOM, LEFT TO RIGHT:
FIG. 4: Wood roof slats, ceremonial gate, Kinkakuji, Kyoto, Japan, seventeenth century

FIG. 5: Bjorklunden, Door County, Wisconsin, 1947, modeled after a stave church in Lillehammer, Norway
FIG. 6: Todaiji Temple, Nara, Japan, eighth century

to decay or burn leaves few remaining examples of old wood structures. The transubstantiation of wood architecture into stone—as well as ancient pictorial and written descriptions of wood construction—provides clues about early building practices in wood.

The earliest recorded use of wood dates back to 20,000 BCE, when modified tree trunks were used to support prehistoric dwellings. European log building techniques originated around 9000 BCE. The Egyptians used wood for furniture and coffins prior to 2500 BCE, and the Greeks and Romans used wood extensively for the construction of boats, bridges, buildings, chariots, and furniture before 1 CE.

Despite the predominance of the use of stone in large landmark edifices, the material used for building of grand scale was not limited to stone. The development of sophisticated timber-framing techniques allowed the construction of impressive and enduring structures in wood as well. The Norwegian stave churches of the eleventh to thirteenth centuries and Japanese temples—such as the eighth-century Todaiji temple in Nara, which remains the largest wooden structure in the world—are examples. [**FIGS. 5+6**]

Wood was imported into regions lacking dense forests during the Middle Ages, and the need for this transport encouraged efficient use of the material. In addition to architecture, timber-framing methods were applied in the building of large-scale structures like bridges, towers, and dams. Wood remained the dominant material of engineering until the seventeenth century.[4]

Today, wood is most commonly used in small-scale and residential construction. Interestingly, the modern wood frame has evolved with an internal contradiction: the framing members themselves are not strong enough to resist shear loads; therefore, the skin must be of adequate rigidity. This interdependency between structure and skin is a distinctive feature of wood construction, and architects often blur the two. As a result, wood may be used to express multiple meanings: strength and delicacy, heft and lightness, depth and surface.

Modern Precedents
The industrial revolution led to the mass production of highly engineered building components, including

WOOD

lumber, tailored for specific functions. While this development facilitated the rapid construction of small-scale buildings, such as single-family residences, it also gave birth to an industry focused more on expediency than innovation. Notable modern works of wood architecture, therefore, are those that have purposefully exploited the particular strengths of the material—such as warmth, lightness, and sculptural fluidity—beyond the conventional modes of wood construction.

The house that Frank Lloyd Wright designed for Herbert and Katherine Jacobs in 1936 is modest in scale yet bold in its aspirations. [**FIG. 7**] The Jacobs House embodies Wright's vision for the future of domestic construction, manifesting the full potential offered by the industrialization of timber. The design of the house is based on a precise set of modules originating from a 2 x 4 foot (0.6 x 1.2 M) grid, and its walls and roof consist of minimal substance, representing the ultimate reduction of material. The walls have no frame and are made of vertical pine boards sandwiched between horizontal cedar battens, resulting in a previously inconceivable thinness of 2½ inches

(6.35 CM). [**FIG. 8**] The alternating striped patterns in the walls and ceiling are more reminiscent of the application of tent fabric than of vernacular timber construction. [**FIG. 9**]

Aligning with Wright's philosophy of organic architecture, Alvar Aalto sought a more humane aesthetic for what he perceived to be an increasingly mechanical treatment of wood.[5] This aesthetic highlighted the inherent warmth and tactility of wood—as well as the plastic qualities Aalto had realized in hisbent plywood furniture—with the goal "to give life a gentler structure."[6] Aalto's celebrated Finnish Pavilion for the 1939 New York World's Fair expressed not only the warmth and tactility of timber but also its monumental grandeur. [**FIGS. 10+11**] As visitors entered the simple, rectilinear structure, they immediately encountered the nearly 52 feet (16 m) tall serpentine wall, constructed of vertical wood strips intermittently overlaid with photographs of Finnish industrial production. The multitiered, undulating surface leaned dramatically outward, as if to emphasize the majesty and instability of the primeval Finnish forest.

Fay Jones's Thorncrown Chapel celebrates the grandeur as well as delicacy of wood. [**FIG.12**] Built in 1980 in a forest near Eureka Springs, Arkansas, the 24 foot wide x 60 foot long x 48 foot tall (7.32 x 18.29 x 14.63 m) structure appears to be much larger than its intimate size. From a fieldstone foundation springs an intricate network of thin filigree of standard wood members, which were delivered on foot to the remote site. The interior volume is defined by a closely spaced sequence of lattice structures that recall both Gothic edifices as well as the surrounding forest, which is clearly visible beyond the 6,000 square foot (557.42 m²) glass facade. [**FIG.13**] Enhancing the seeming fragility of the chapel are the central intersection points of the wood members, which are articulated as voids where one expects solidity.

Environmental Considerations

Wood is a renewable material and a completely recyclable biological nutrient. Its tissue is a product of water carrying trace elements from the soil and of carbon dioxide from the air. With the assistance of chlorophyll and sunlight, biomass is formed and oxygen is released. Wood contains about 50 percent carbon, which remains in the timber until it decays or is burned—at which time carbon dioxide, water, and energy are released. For this reason forests and wood products act as significant global carbon sinks. The forests of Europe alone store twenty times the carbon dioxide emitted into the atmosphere annually.[7] Advocates of carbon sequestration argue that wood building materials not only extend this

storage capacity but also compare favorably with concrete or metal, which emit carbon dioxide during their production.

Forests cover nearly one-third of Earth's land area. [**FIG.14**] In recent decades forest-covered zones have been increasing in developed countries by 3 percent while decreasing at a rate of 9 percent in developing nations.[8] The modern practice of forestry management has been adopted extensively to maintain healthy and productive forests as well as to reduce the levels of deforestation in developing countries. Inspired by the sustainability principle set forth by accountant and mining administrator Hans Carl von Carlowitz in his 1713 treatise *Sylvicultura Oeconomica* (Silvicultural economics) and later ratified in the 1987 Brundtland Report by the World Commission on Environment and Development (established by the United Nations Environment Program), forestry management involves origin and chain-of-custody certification systems that minimize the illegal harvesting of timber and assure the renewability of forests.[9] Forest-certification programs in current use internationally are operated by organizations including the Forest Stewardship Council (FSC), the Programme for the Endorsement of Forest Certification schemes (PEFC), the American Tree Farm System (ATFS), the Canadian Standards Association (CSA), and the Sustainable Forestry Initiative (SFI).

Despite concerns about deforestation, environmentalists generally advocate the use of wood-based building products since they do not require much energy for their manufacture and compare favorably

WOOD

FIG.16: Platform framing in residential construction, Katy, Texas

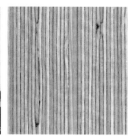

with other energy-intensive building materials. The harvesting, milling, drying, and transport of wood results in a low embodied energy, and the economic investment is relatively low as well—wood is one of the most plentiful and least expensive raw materials. [**FIG.15**]

The modern industrialization of timber and the depletion of old growth forests have resulted in an increased quantity of engineered lumber products made from lesser-grade materials. [**FIG.16**] Although wood structural members in preindustrial buildings were typically made directly from mature trees, today they consist of multiple, smaller pieces of younger wood held in place with glue. [**FIG.17**] Modern laminated-veneer lumber, plywood, and particleboard contain higher percentages of glue and filler materials than prior lumber products and, as a result, are less able to accommodate the shrinking and swelling that results from moisture penetration and water-vapor diffusion. Contemporary wood construction is thus characterized by tight construction tolerances, because the slightest error in building-envelope detailing can lead to mold growth and decay in engineered-wood materials. Also, toxic coatings must be carefully controlled or avoided, as some preservatives, sealants, and paints used to extend the life of wood products are carcinogenic and may off-gas into interior environments.

The increased demand for regenerative resources in recent years has encouraged manufacturers to make building products from rapidly renewable sources, like bamboo, sorghum, and wheat, which may be grown and harvested within shorter time frames than most timber species. New biocomposites are also being developed from wood fibers and resins with recycled-fiber reinforcement and are considered mutant materials in that they are made from wood yet behave like plastic—the ultimate fulfillment of technological control.

Disruptive Technologies

In architectural practice as well as in the academic study, wood is the most common building material given its predominant use in small-scale construction, furniture fabrication, and model making (the reason model shops are often called wood shops). The benefits and drawbacks of conventional wood-working are therefore widely understood. However, recent advances in wood and wood-based technologies reveal a broad and fundamental transformation underway, precipitated by an intensifying interest in renewable resources and enhancement of material performance.

Wood's susceptibility to decay is well known, and various preservation methods have been developed to limit deterioration in wood used for building construction. A pressure-impregnation process using coal-tar creosote (a wood preservative) developed in 1838 by inventor John Bethell remains the primary method for pressure treating lumber today.[10] However, because coal-tar creosote and other common preservatives are carcinogenic and do not decay quickly in groundwater, they are subject to increased regulatory control.

FIG. 18: Kebonized high performance wood by Kebony ASA

FIG. 19: Three-dimensional formable wood veneer by Reholz GmbH

FIG. 20: Sculptured Collection 3D-milled integral-color medium density fiberboard (MDF) and wood-veneer panels by Architectural Systems, Inc.

67

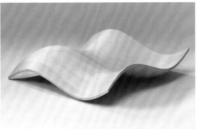
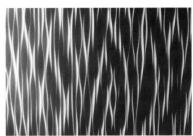

Fortunately, more environmentally responsible methods have been developed to enhance the durability of wood. Acetylated wood is a long-lasting, solid wood that is created by chemically converting the cellular structure of the wood to make it hydrophobic, which avoids the need to impregnate the wood cells with toxic substances. This transformation reduces decay, swelling, shrinking, UV degradation, and vulnerability to insects and mold. Kebonization is another method used to preserve wood with a less environmentally damaging process. [**FIG. 18**] Biowaste from the sugar industry is converted into a liquid that is used to strengthen the cellular walls of the wood, making it harder and denser than untreated wood. This irreversible process bonds the liquid polymer permanently to the wood, reducing shrinkage and swelling by 50 percent.

Other methods have been developed to yield wood with unprecedented flexibility. Inventor Christian Luther's development of the hot-plate press in 1896 made curvilinear forms in plywood readily achievable.[11] A century later inventor Achim Möller developed a molding process for veneer that enables the precise fabrication of sophisticated compound-curved geometries that were previously impossible. [**FIG. 19**] Bendywood, a form of pliable wood manufactured by Candidus Prugger in Italy, is created by steaming and compressing solid wood along its length, creating wood that can easily be bent to a radius as small as ten times its thickness when cold and dry. Since no chemicals are added, the process is environmentally superior to traditional wood

bending or laminating techniques. Other techniques enable the fabrication of elaborate geometries for striking visual effect as well as for enhanced acoustic performance. [**FIG. 20**]

Increasingly widespread computer-controlled-fabrication processes, like laser cutting and CNC milling, enable manufacturing to occur at the site of construction, which reduces transportation energy and time. Several manufacturers have embraced this trend with new composite panels designed exclusively for digital-fabrication processes. These panels are typically composed of wood veneers laminated to lightweight core materials, allowing for precise laser-driven cuts and score lines. Other digital treatments enable the application of images and other graphic content to wood and cellulose fiber–based materials.

Anticipated shortages in petroleum have shifted demand toward renewable resources; and as competition increases for wood products and as forestry practices are scrutinized with greater intensity, manufacturers have become keen on developing alternative cellulosic materials to augment current timber supplies. In less than a decade, bamboo, appreciated for its rapid growth and higher material yield per area compared with trees, has quickly become a popular alternative to hardwood as a finish material. Bamboo paneling is dense and strong, and may be used in a variety of woodworking applications. Unfortunately, bamboo's popularity has encouraged deforestation in some countries, so it is important to select an environmentally responsible supplier.

WOOD

Manufacturers have also developed building products made from agricultural materials such as the inedible parts of wheat or sorghum, because these materials are grown more rapidly than trees and would normally be treated as waste. Examples of application include decorative panels used as alternatives to wood veneers and structural insulated panels (SIP) made of oriented strand board (OSB) laminated to a core of compressed agricultural fibers that provide thermal insulation. Another alternative cellulosic material is derived from invasive-plant species that grow rapidly and aggressively and displace indigenous plants. Manufacturers can remove these parasitic plants from affected areas and use them in new building products and furniture.

Another breed of cellulosic products is a hybrid between wood and plastic. This material possesses properties similar to wood but may be injection molded like plastic. In one process, natural wood is infused with acrylic resin to create a more durable, dimensionally stable material that resists dents and water penetration. [**FIG. 21**] Another process combines waste lignin from the paper industry, natural fibers (such as hemp, flax, or wood), and additives such as wax to create thermoplastic granules that then may be melted or injection molded. Manufacturers of plasticized-wood products claim that these goods enable abundant softwoods to replace scarcer hardwoods typically used in finishing and help reduce dependence on petroleum-derived polymers. [**FIG. 22**]

Disruptive Applications

The development of stronger, lighter, and more-durable wood products parallels the technological trajectory of all construction materials. Although building codes often restrict the use of wood in fire-resistant-building construction, architects have imagined bold applications of wood in the wake of the anticipated "carbohydrate economy."[12] For the Mannheim Multihalle exhibition space (1975), for example, Frei Otto and Buro Happold designed a large-span timber gridshell made of a wood lattice. The timber mesh was fabricated on the ground and raised in place to make a double-curved shell. Tezuka Architects created a spatial lattice in Woods of Net (2009), a pavilion for the Hakone Open-Air Museum in Japan. Nearly six hundred large-timber beams are stacked to create a partially enclosed, irregular dome spanning an area over 1,700 square feet (520 m²) without the use of metal reinforcing.

Architects have also been eager to test limits using other renewable, wood-alternative materials like paper and bamboo. Shigeru Ban's many works made from paper tubes demonstrate the surprising structural capacity of this "weak" material. Ban's Paper Tower for the 2009 London Design Festival employed cardboard tubes manufactured by Sonoco to make a 72 foot (22 m) high conical construction—the tallest paper tower in existence. [**FIG. 23**] Kengo Kuma & Associates' Great (Bamboo) Wall house (2002) outside of Beijing incorporates light-filtering layers of regularly spaced bamboo—an application that creates the illusion that this sturdy material is delicate

TOP, LEFT TO RIGHT:
FIG. 24: Kengo Kuma & Associates, Great (Bamboo) Wall, Beijing, China, 2002

FIG. 25: Miguel Arruda, Habitable Sculpture, Lisbon, Portugal, 2010, interior showing cork cladding

BOTTOM, LEFT TO RIGHT:
FIG. 26: Gramazio & Kohler, ETH Zurich, Sequential Wall, 2008. Students: Milena Isler, Morten Krog, Ellen Leuenberger, Steffen Samberger.

FIG. 27: Issho Architects, Yufutoku Restaurant, Tokyo, Japan, 2009, detail of exterior vertical louvers

69

WOOD

and weightless. [FIG. 24] Miguel Arruda's *Habitable Sculpture* tests the surface-wrapping capacity of cork, which encloses both the interior and exterior of a pavilion for the Lisbon Architectural Triennale (2010). [FIG. 25]

New digitally controlled milling and fabrication processes have facilitated the realization of complex geometries in wood construction with increased precision. Gramazio & Kohler's *Sequential Wall* installations in Zurich (2008) reveal the application of generative, software-driven parameters on collections of wooden slats. [FIG. 26] The intricately stacked wood members create complex, undulating surfaces that address aesthetic as well as structural and environmental considerations—they channel water like pine needles or fish scales. Issho Architects' Yufutoku Restaurant (2009) in Tokyo incorporates evenly spaced, vertical wooden louvers of varying widths, resulting in a rippled surface that filters light between the exterior and the interior of the restaurant. [FIG. 27] The Wave Wall in Snøhetta's Oslo Opera House (2007) is another visually striking surface, made of finished oak strips of different depths and profiles.

With its rich texture, the wall invokes the traditions of Norwegian shipbuilding and musical instrument crafting. (See pages 60–61.)

Unique finish treatments characterize another group of recent wood applications in architecture— from novel surface coatings to hybrid material composites. Tham & Videgård Hansson Arkitekter's House K (2004) in Stockholm, for example, makes use of super-scaled "shingles" made of black stained plywood, which denies the natural color of the material but subtly reveals its surface grain. In his Yakisugi House (2006) in Nagano, Terunobu Fujimori intentionally burned the cedar slats applied vertically to the facade. The result is a visually striking surface that has been completely charred in order to preserve the wood while also giving it a rich black color and texture. Diller Scofidio + Renfro collaborated with 3form to create a heat-formable composite using wood for the interior walls of Alice Tully Hall (2009) in New York. The result is a moldable material that combines resin and wood veneer, and reveals an unexpected translucency when backlit.

Stadthaus

London, United Kingdom
Waugh Thistleton Architects
2007

Waugh Thistleton's Stadthaus is the world's tallest residential building made of timber. A nine-story, twenty-nine-unit tower located in the Murray Grove neighborhood of London, the Stadthaus is constructed almost exclusively of cross-laminated timber (CLT), a hypersized, structural plywood. CLT adapts the model of veneers laminated in an alternating cross-grain pattern to maximize lateral strength and increases the possible scale of the load-bearing sheets to a story high. Rather that using veneers, the engineered panels are made of rows of spruce strips layered in alternating orientations and glued under pressure. The result is a product that may be used vertically or horizontally, for walls, floors, and even structural cores of the building.

The impetus to use wood originated with its carbon-storage capacity. According to the architects, the Stadthaus's 12,000 cubic yards (9,175 m³) of timber sequester 186 tons of carbon dioxide, which will remain stored in the material throughout the building's lifespan.

Waugh Thistleton demonstrated an adequate fire-resistance rating of ninety minutes (the time period during which a material can withstand a standard fire-resistance test) for the timber assembly, noting that wood also forms a self-preserving layer of char when burned that increases this time frame. The prefabricated CLT panels were assembled on-site using platform construction and connected with simple screws and angle plates. The building's multicolored facade is made of composite panels made of 70 percent waste wood pulp and 30 percent fiber cement.

WOOD

Final Wooden House

Kumamoto, Japan
Sou Fujimoto
2008

For his entry to the 2005 competition entitled Next Generation Wooden Bungalows, Sou Fujimoto sought to test the versatility of wood construction. Rather than employing engineered lumber in its various specialized formats tailored to different uses—such as for framing, trim, or sheathing—the architect selected a single format that could satisfy different functions based on spatial position. The resulting Final Wooden House is a cube-shaped structure made entirely of 14 inch (35 cm) sided timber pieces of different lengths that are stacked and staggered to create a nested, cavelike volume. The house embodies Fujimoto's interest in creating a primitive architecture using the simplest elements—a reinterpretation of the early hut.

Although there is essentially only one type of building block used in the house, the experiential character of Final Wooden House inspires endless functional interpretations: the timber modules serve not only as walls, beams, floor, and ceiling, but also as benches, desks, and bookshelves. Fujimoto's 161 square foot (15 m²) construction presents an intricately wrought plan while freeing the section, inviting the user to establish programmatic variety based on the shifting relationship between the body and the architecture. This intimate relationship ultimately takes advantage of the haptic sensibility of wood as a material.

OPPOSITE: Interior showing stacked timbers of uniform width

TOP: Exterior
BOTTOM LEFT: Timber location and spacing suggests multiple functions.

BOTTOM RIGHT: Interior view showing multiple implied levels

73

WOOD

Sclera Pavilion

London, United Kingdom
Adjaye Associates
2008

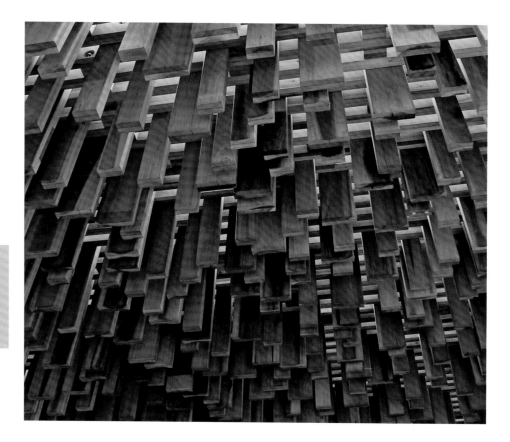

Wood's fibrous tissue often inspires associations with the cells of the human skin, but with Sclera Pavilion the operative metaphor is the eye. Designed as a temporary pavilion for the 2008 London Design Festival, Sclera is a porous cylindrical chamber, a public space where visitors can experience the modulation of light through a complex spatial assembly of tulipwood.

A wood species native to North America, American tulipwood accounts for 9 percent of hardwood production and exhibits a strength-to-weight ratio superior to many other hardwoods. With the pavilion David Adjaye sought to test not only the material's structural durability and weight but also its ability to withstand abuse from the elements and a high volume of human traffic.

Nearly fourteen hundred pieces of engineered American tulipwood function as structure, walls, ornamentation, and atmosphere—establishing both a seamlessness and an indeterminacy between support and cladding, surface and frame. Nine hundred twenty vertical strips hang precariously from the ceiling, suggesting an inverted urban topography or a massive wood chandelier. The use of prefabricated structural modules, which were constructed off-site over a six-week period, minimized the time required for installation to eight days.

Spanish Pavilion

Shanghai, China
EMBT
2010

EMBT designed Spain's pavilion for the 2010 Shanghai Expo to have a visually arresting display of an experimental cladding made of woven wicker panels fastened to a tubular steel frame. The elaborate geometry of the facade creates the effect of a hovering tidal wave primed to crash onto the streetscape below. The 64,600 square foot (6,000 m²) building was designed as an homage to the traditional handicraft of making wicker baskets (and the material used) common to both Spain and China—an insightful acknowledgment of the countries' similarities. More than eight thousand beige, brown, and black panels were made by hand by artisans in Shandong province, and each panel is unique.

The unusual combination of a robust steel frame and natural reed mat-panels creates a visual vibration—the nondefined, blurry edges of the building drift in and out of focus. Technically, this pairing cleverly allows the wicker panels to twist and contort naturally based on their own inherent mechanical properties—in contrast to the hermetically fitted, individually customized metal panels on Frank Gehry–designed buildings. This match allows structure and skin to be simultaneously integrated and distinct, and the envelope allows varying degrees of light and view penetration.

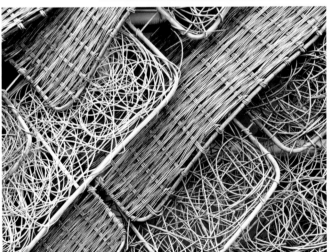

2049 Pavilion

Shanghai, China
Zhu Jianping, China Vanke Co. Ltd.
2010

Vanke, one of the largest property developers in China, constructed a pavilion at the Shanghai Expo entitled 2049, referring to the centennial year of the People's Republic of China. The sustainability themed building is composed of seven independent, truncated cones. Surrounded by a large moat of water, this collection of monolithic forms appears imposing from a distance.

The most striking aspect of the 2049 pavilion is not its shape but its clever use of material. From afar the great expanse of small-scale, horizontal lines on the facade seem to be beige-colored brick. As one nears the structure, the fact that the "bricks" overlap one another, in a relationship that suggests ceramic tiles, becomes obvious. In reality, the pavilion is clad with tile-size panels made of wheat straw.

This material application demonstrates the extent to which borrowing the common scale and pattern of another material assembly can surprise and provoke. Like brick, the narrow wheat-straw boards soften the scale of the massive volumes and provides a pleasing golden color to the facade. But unlike brick the straw panels are incredibly lightweight, and require no mining and much less energy to manufacture.

OPPOSITE: Interior at night
TOP LEFT: View of pavilion
exterior with moat

TOP RIGHT: Wheat straw tiles
possess a haptic quality absent
in brick or ceramic tiles.
BOTTOM: Interior galleries

81

WOOD

METAL

METAL

Our hearts were filled with an immense pride at feeling ourselves standing quite alone, like lighthouses or like the sentinels in an outpost, facing the army of enemy stars encamped in their celestial bivouacs. Alone with the engineers in the infernal stokeholes of great ships, alone with the black spirits which rage in the belly of rogue locomotives, alone with the drunkards beating their wings against the walls. — Filippo Tommaso Marinetti

Metal is the material most explicitly identified with periods of human civilization: the Silver Age, Bronze Age, or Iron Age, for example. Throughout history, metal has symbolized modernization—from early bronze tools to the amorphous metals resulting from nanotechnological experiments, metals have propelled the advancement of society. As the primary material feedstock of the industrial revolution, metal represents both the headlong, relentless drive toward industrial development as well as the realization of technological sophistication and refinement. When adopted too swiftly, industrialization has produced adverse human-health and environmental effects—as seen in Victorian England or during China's Great Leap Forward campaign. However, the outcomes of industrialization are increased economic growth, technological utility, and cultural transformation. Architectural critic Reyner Banham states that while "the machinery of the preceding Victorian Industrial Age of 'cast iron, soot and rust' had been ponderous, simple-minded, tended by a mass-proletariat in parts of the world that were remote from centers of enlightenment and culture, [the gleaming steel-forged] machines of the First Machine Age of the early twentieth century were light, subtle, clean, and could be handled by thinking men in their own homes out in the new electric suburbs."[1]

Throughout the ages, metal has exemplified both strength and beauty—two fundamental aspirations of human civilization. Early bronze weapons and modern steel freighters epitomize strength and demonstrate mankind's desire to conquer and control. Ancient gold jewelry and present-day gilded electronic devices—two representations of status and sophistication—embody the idea of beauty. Together the qualities of strength and beauty have come to represent material progress, and historians assess a society's level of advancement in part based on its use of metal. Manifested in threatening machines of war or extravagantly high-tech automobiles, the idea of achievement today often remains connected to the material sublimity of metal.

The search for strength and beauty likewise motivates the use of metal in architecture, in both the application as building structure and as skin. From wide-flange steel columns to ornamental filigree, metal has exhibited broad versatility as a building material and epitomizes both the rawness and grace described by Banham. [FIGS.1-3]

Composition

Metals make up the bulk of the periodic table of the elements and display a broad range of qualities. They are defined as crystalline structures with free electrons, and exhibit good conductivity, reflectivity,

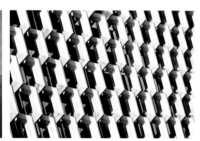

and opacity. When compared with other materials, metals exhibit high levels of density, strength, stiffness, and weight. Metals are also ductile and therefore can be readily molded using processes such as rolling and extrusion. With the exception of noble metals like gold and platinum, all metals are chemically unstable—they easily corrode (give off free electrons) to form more stable compounds when they come in contact with nonmetallic elements, like oxygen. Thus, metals require special coatings and maintenance to resist corrosion—although copper, aluminum, zinc, and lead form their own protective surface coatings (patina) during the preliminary stage of corrosion that slows down subsequent deterioration.[2] [**FIGS. 4+5**]

Metals are typically distinguished as being ferrous or nonferrous (containing iron or not). Iron-based alloys, like steel, are particularly important for building construction (steel accounts for more than 90 percent of global metal consumption, followed by aluminum, copper, nickel, zinc, titanium, magnesium, and tungsten).[3] Because most metals used in building construction are alloys, pure metals must first be extracted from ores, like sulfides and carbonates,

before being blended with elements such as carbon or silicon to produce an alloy with the desired performance attributes. Metal may be cold or hot worked as well as machined. Cold working transforms the size or shape of the metal mechanically by plastic deformation, while hot working changes its size or shape by heating it above its recrystallization temperature, which increases its ductility. Conventional metal-processing techniques include casting, forging, rolling, drawing, extruding, twisting, and mechanical machining.[4] [**FIG. 6**]

History

The discovery of metal marks a significant milestone in human civilization, and its early processing from ore roughly parallels the beginning of recorded history. Naturally occurring metals like gold were used in limited fashion for jewelry until around 4300 BCE, and the discovery of extraction and metal-casting techniques in Central Europe at this time marked the beginning of the Copper Age. The development of an alloy of copper and tin around 3500 BCE initiated the Bronze Age, an era in which objects such as weapons,

FIG.7: Sutemi Horiguchi, Koide Residence, Koganei, Japan, 1925, detail of gold-leaf wall designed to amplify interior illumination

FIG.8: Gustave Eiffel, Eiffel Tower, Paris, France, 1889

FIG.9: Shreve, Lamb & Harmon, Empire State Building, New York, New York, 1931

utensils, tools, and jewelry became increasingly commercialized, leading to the development of organized trading and more advanced social systems. The Iron Age began around 1400 BCE, when the more common iron ore was harnessed despite the processing challenges it posed.

The process of mining is directly connected with the material itself—the word *metal* originates from the Greek *metallon*, which means "mine" or "quarry." According to historian Charles Stelman, Greek metal workers were highly respected for their ability to transform raw ore into objects of beauty: "Even in the distant age of bronze the inhabitants of Greece and the islands held the skilled worker in metal in very high regard. His art was both a mystery and a delight, and he was thought to owe his gifts to supernatural beings around whom many legends grew."[5]

One of the first applications of metal in architecture consisted of the small and inconspicuous cramps used to hold together stones in Greek edifices (circa 500 BCE). Over time, however, metal began to play an increasingly substantive and conspicuous role. Aesthetically, metal had long been appreciated for its reflective properties and was symbolically associated with light because of its ability to brighten dark interiors. [**FIG.7**] Structurally, metal began to replace wood and stone with the application of cast iron in the nineteenth century. First utilized in bridges and industrial structures, cast iron enjoyed increasing prominence and technological sophistication in buildings such as Henri Labrouste's St. Geneviève library (1850), Joseph Paxton's The Crystal Palace

(1851), and Gustave Eiffel's tower for the 1889 international expo in Paris. [**FIG.8**]

Steel was introduced in 1855, and the Bessemer process—the first cost-effective industrial process for the mass production of steel from molten pig iron—made large-scale steel production possible.[6] The opportune combination of the advent of the steel frame and the elevator with rising land prices in cities like New York and Chicago led to the development of the skyscraper toward the end of the nineteenth century. These so-called cathedrals of commerce began to dominate the American skyline by the turn of the century, and in 1931 a steel frame supported the 102 stories of Shreve, Lamb & Harmon's Empire State Building—a feat of engineering that remained the world's tallest building for four decades. [**FIG.9**]

Metal dramatically shaped society in the twentieth century. As architect and writer Annette LeCuyer describes: "In architecture, as in the daily lives of consumers, metals and modernity were inseparable. Modernist preoccupations with the skeletal frame and the curtain wall generated the free plan, ideas of universal space, and experiments with mass-produced buildings."[7]

Modern Precedents

A survey of modern applications of metal in architecture reveals a fascination with industrial production and technological advancement. Embracing the machine aesthetic, architects utilized exposed-metal structures and cladding for institutions and residences—functions that had previously been

fulfilled by masonry, wood, or earthen materials. This unusual treatment marked the attempt to appropriate the vigor and hyperfunctionality of the machine in the search of a new level of refinement and sophistication in architecture. [**FIG.10**]

Mies van der Rohe's architectural tour-de-force, Farnsworth House, situated astride the Fox River south of Plano, Illinois, is an essay that subverts the unstable relationship between man and machine. [**FIG.11**] Designed for Dr. Edith Farnsworth and exhibited in model form at the Museum of Modern Art in 1947, the house is a modernist masterpiece and one of the most iconic architectural works of the twentieth century. Constructed of a carefully fabricated steel frame with a precast-concrete slab and floor-to-ceiling glass windows, the building consists of two horizontal planes that define a single, continuous space of habitation that appears to float above the landscape. Mies chose to minimize the visual presence of structural connections and to sandblast, prime, and paint the trabeated skeleton white after erection—a strategy that imparted a visual elegance and ephemerality to the building. Although the client would find the house difficult to occupy because of the lack of privacy, the Farnsworth House is regarded as one of Mies's most thoughtful attempts to join the advances of mass industrialization with the newfound freedoms of the individual.

Taking the aesthetics of mass industrialization to new heights, the winning competition entry that Renzo Piano and Richard Rogers submitted for the design of Centre Georges Pompidou in 1971 jolted the art world. [**FIG.12**] By celebrating the building's structural and mechanical systems as colorful facade elements suspended within an exposed three-dimensional lattice, Piano and Rogers furnished a machine in which to house art. Constructed in 1977 in the Beaubourg neighborhood of Paris, the 1 million square foot (100,000 m²) building was designed to be "a flexible container and dynamic communications machine" made of prefabricated components.[8] Visible facade elements include cast-steel columns, massive "gerberettes" (cantilevered beams), and post-tension bracing, as well as color-coded piping for plumbing, mechanical, electrical, and fire safety services.[9] When Rogers won the Pritzker Architecture Prize in 2007, the jury claimed that the Pompidou had "revolutionized museums, transforming what had once been elite monuments into popular places of social and cultural exchange, woven into the heart of the city."[10]

Two decades later the construction of Frank Gehry's design for the Guggenheim Museum (1997) in Bilbao demonstrated the power of architecture to influence urban identity. Situated on a former shipyard in a gritty city that was reeling from the failure of its shipbuilding and metalworks industries, the 257,000 square foot (23,900 m²) museum, clad in titanium, limestone, and glass, presented a transformational image for Bilbao. The soaring, wavelike forms of the elevation fronting the Nervion River are reminiscent of the city's shipbuilding heritage, and the thousands of luminous titanium panels that cover a majority of the facade reflect the colors of the sky but also set the building apart from its context.

METAL

FIG.13: Gehry, Guggenheim
Museum, Bilbao, Spain, 1997

FIG.14: Century-base-metal
mine, SHMS deposit,
Queensland, Australia

FIG.15: Cyanide heap leaching
of gold ore, Elko, Nevada

[**FIG.13**] The startling visual effect suggests a phoenix-like rebirth of this dispirited city and celebrates the transformation of an industrial metal culture to a postindustrial one—or what Banham has character-ized as the shift from a dirty industrial hub to a center of enlightenment.[11]

Environmental Considerations

Mining is an environmentally unsettling and resource-consuming activity that can cause erosion, biodiversity loss, and soil and groundwater contami-nation. [**FIG.14**] Significant quantities of earth are displaced and existing ecosystems disturbed in the search for usable ore deposits. This overburden is calculated as part of the "ecological rucksack" (the total amount of material displaced to make a product but not used in the product itself).[12] Depending on the metal, the amount of dislodged raw material can be significant—for example, obtaining 1 kilogram of aluminum requires the displacement of 85 kilo-grams of bauxite. Gold is especially resource intensive at a ratio of 1:540,000.[13]

The extraction of metal compounds from ore—called heap leaching—is a toxic process involving the use of cyanide. [**FIG.15**] A more environmentally friendly method called bioleaching utilizes bacteria or fungi to separate precious metals from ore, but this procedure requires more time.

Metal production is also notoriously energy-intensive. Many metals demand twice the energy in primary production (made from ore rather than from recycled scrap) as common plastics per unit weight:

for example, the embodied energy of aluminum is about 220 MJ/kg versus 96 MJ/kg for ABS plastic.[14] The use of metal has also been a significant factor in modern society's nearly complete dependence upon nonrenewable materials.

Due to the massive production of metal during the last century, known stores of common minerals are rapidly diminishing. According to the United States Geological Survey, less than two decades' worth of economically recoverable reserves of lead and tin remain—and only twenty-two years of copper, fifty years of iron ore, and sixty-five years of bauxite.[15]

Some metals are harmful to humans and other living creatures. In particular, toxic-heavy metals, such as lead, mercury, and cadmium, must be carefully regulated. Of the sixteen most hazardous substances to human health identified by the United States Environmental Protection Agency's 35/50 Program in 1988, seven are metals and their compounds.[16] However, other metals such as stainless steel, titanium alloys, and cobalt alloys are safe enough to implant in the human body.[17]

Thermal bridging can be a challenge when using metal in building envelopes, and conduction between exterior and interior components needs to be mini-mized, particularly in extreme climates. Metal also has a high coefficient of thermal expansion and is readily affected by radiant heat. This property can be advanta-geous from an energy-harnessing standpoint, such as in the application of metal-clad solar-thermal collectors. Metal is also the primary structural mate-rial used for the fabrication of renewable-energy

FIG.16: Microtruss-sandwiched periodic cellular material by Cellular Materials International, Inc.

FIG.17: Zinc foam developed by the Fraunhofer Institute

FIG.18: Alkemi composite made from recycled aluminum scrap and resin by Renewed Materials LLC

89

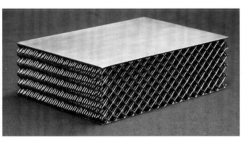
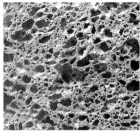

systems, including building-integrated solar- and wind-harnessing technologies.

One of metal's greatest benefits is its recyclability. Unlike many other materials, most metals may be easily recycled with no degradation over time. Moreover, the embodied energy of recycled metals (also called secondary production) is significantly less than that required for primary production—approximately 10 percent for aluminum and 26 percent for stainless steel.[18] The significant environmental and economic advantages of metal recycling will encourage the expansion of closed-loop manufacturing and consumption in which all scraps—considered technical nutrients—are reused to create new materials.[19]

Disruptive Technologies

Advances in metal technology have largely focused on performance enhancement. One aim is higher strength-to-weight ratios, either through improved alloy formulations or more-sophisticated structural shapes. Another goal is to overcome metal's inherent instability by developing longer-wearing surfaces that resist environmental degradation. The focus of particularly intensive research during the mid-twentieth century, metal has evolved significantly and remains a material of choice for some of the most demanding architectural applications.

Due to its high mechanical resilience, metal is a favored material of military and aerospace industries. Metal has demonstrated increased resistance to high-impact loads when configured as a microstructure

made of several layers of different alloys. Composite metal panels called periodic cellular materials (PCM) consist of lightweight metal honeycomb, prism, or lattice structures sandwiched between two sheets. [**FIG.16**] These configurations offer good resistance to blast and ballistic protection in high-security and natural disaster–prone environments. Composite panels come in a wide variety of configurations, such as metal-face-sheets-cladding-extruded polystyrene cores or transparent-polymers-facing metal-honeycomb cores. The development of foamed metals containing a significant volume of air-filled pores has also produced materials with high stiffness, low weight, and high levels of energy absorption. Foamed aluminum and foamed zinc require a minimal level of material for effective impact resistance, electromagnetic shielding, resonance limiting, and acoustic noise reduction—and are also 100 percent recyclable. [**FIG.17**]

Given its high luster and malleability, metal is often put to work in applications requiring sophisticated color, finish, and textural effects. Advanced surfacing composites made from metallic particles and polymeric resin are used for vertical finish treatments. These hybrid surfaces include cast-metal granules in a fiber-reinforced-polymer (FRP) matrix as well as postindustrial scrap metal cast within transparent resin. [**FIG.18**]

Metal is harnessed in a variety of advanced digital-fabrication processes, such as algorithmically derived metal systems made from bending complex shapes in sheet metal. These shapes enhance mechanical

METAL

FIG. 19: XURF Systems continuously morphable, curved sheet metal surfaces by Milgo/Bufkin

FIG. 20: Photo-engraved aluminum panels by Intaglio Composites

FIG. 21: Herzog & de Meuron and Ai Wei-Wei, Beijing National Stadium, Beijing, China, 2008

performance as well as visual interest and serve as economical alternatives to extrusions and roll forming. [**FIG. 19**] Another digital application involves the transfer of graphic material onto a metal surface. Photoengraving allows the permanent transfer of photographic data, such as halftone images or vector graphics, to the surface of metal panels for exterior-grade use. [**FIG. 20**] These panels may be flat, convex, concave, or compound-curved, and the etching depth may be varied.

One of the more intriguing advances in metals is the development of shape memory. Scientists William Buehler and Frederick Wang discovered this property in 1962 in an alloy of equal parts nickel and titanium. Called nitinol, in homage to its place of origin, Nickel Titanium Naval Ordnance Laboratory, the alloy exhibits both shape memory and super-elasticity.[20] Nitinol's ability to "remember" its original shape when heated after being deformed has made it a popular material for inclusion in biomedical devices, couplings, actuators, and sensors. Researchers are experimenting with shape memory alloys (SMA) in the development of active shading systems for buildings, which could be used to reduce solar heat gain because of their ability to transform based on changes in environmental stimuli.

Disruptive Applications

Metal continues to define significant future trajectories for architecture. Although the Age of Steel experienced its apogee during the twentieth century, emerging digital technologies continue to transform metal production today. Structural engineers now use sophisticated software to calculate complex assemblies that would not have been built during prior decades due to their structural indeterminacy. [**FIG. 21**] Based on these advanced simulation capabilities, architects and engineers can collaborate closely in search of an enhanced design authenticity that expresses the performance of a building in its form. This integrated approach seeks a visual expression for a building's structural-loading diagram that reveals the different sizes and frequencies of structural members necessary for the efficient use of materials. During the construction process, metal components may be fabricated precisely using computer-controlled machinery that ensures a high level of quality while minimizing waste.

Because metal is used heavily in industries that fabricate large-scale constructions—such as aerospace and shipbuilding—it is possible to transfer technical advances achieved by these trades to architecture. When the Japanese shipbuilding industry fell on hard times during the 1980s, for example, architecture found an unlikely partner for the construction of sophisticated buildings. According to shipbuilder Kazushi Takahashi, "the basic science behind [architecture and shipbuilding], the arithmetic and physics, are the same."[21] Shipbuilders played an instrumental role in constructing important contemporary metal buildings, such as Toyo Ito & Associates' Sendai Mediatheque (2001) and Nikken Sekkei Ltd.'s Jinbocho Theater in Tokyo (2008). [**FIG. 22**] Like the increasingly commonplace

TOP, LEFT TO RIGHT:

FIG. 22: Nikken Sekkei Ltd., Jinbocho Theater, Tokyo, Japan, 2008, detail of exterior cladding

FIG. 23: Herzog & de Meuron, M. H. de Young Memorial Museum, San Francisco, California, 2005
FIG. 24: Atelier Hitoshi Abe, Aoba-tei Restaurant, Sendai, Japan, 2005

BOTTOM, LEFT TO RIGHT:
FIG. 25: Hiroshi Nakamura & NAP, Lanvin Boutique Ginza store, Tokyo, Japan, 2004, exterior detail

FIG. 26: Inaba Electric Works, Eco-Curtain, Nagoya, Japan, 2005
FIG. 27: Ned Kahn, *Wind Veil* at Target Field, Minneapolis, Minnesota, 2010

91

collaboration with structural engineers, the new working relationships with shipbuilders have allowed architects to facilitate the blurring of structure and skin—as well as the merging of the various surfaces of walls, roofs, and floors in buildings.

Metal's versatility as a material makes it a prime candidate for new explorations in surface pattern and texture, as seen in the nature-inspired surface treatments in buildings like Herzog & de Meuron's de Young Museum (2005) in San Francisco or Atelier Hitoshi Abe's Aoba-tei restaurant (2005) in Sendai. [**FIGS. 23+24**] Metal can also be made to mimic other materials like fabric, as in Herzog & de Meuron's Walker Art Center addition (2005) in Minneapolis. Patterns can also result from abstract combinations of two materials. Hiroshi Nakamura & NAP's Lanvin Boutique Ginza store (2004) in Tokyo, for example, incorporates solid acrylic cylinders as apertures within honeycomb structural steel plates. [**FIG. 25**] During fabrication, the acrylic cylinders were inserted into the steel at minus 30°C, and as the assembly thawed on-site, the two materials expanded to create a weather-tight seal.[22]

With its machine-age legacy, metal is an obvious choice for use in adaptable, mechanized systems. Inaba Electric Works' Eco-Curtain is a wind-harnessing surface that not only powers the lighting within a retail building but also serves as the facade for its structured parking garage—demonstrating the potential of building-integrated renewable-energy technologies. [**FIG. 26**] Other approaches include surfaces that actively respond to environmental phenomena. Ned Kahn's *Wind Veil* installation (2010) at Target Field in Minneapolis, for example, utilizes thousands of freely rotating aluminum micropanels that respond to moving air currents and provide visual expression for the complex morphology of wind. [**FIG. 27**]

METAL

Kanno Museum

Sendai, Japan
Atelier Hitoshi Abe
2006

Commissioned to design a museum for a client's small private collection of art, Hitoshi Abe created a box with a fluid interior landscape inspired by the structure of soap bubbles. Abe designed each gallery to act like an individual bubble within a larger cube, and the surfaces of different bubbles were to intersect to form angled walls and floors in the building. After consulting with a structural engineer and a shipbuilder assigned to the museum project team, Abe decided that the material used for the boundary surfaces would serve as both the structure and skin of the building.

The surfaces are composed of ⅛ inch (3.2 mm) thick steel plates with embossed dimples in a regular grid arrangement. The lozenge-shaped depressions mark the alignment points between paired plates, which are mirrored in plan, to create a strong, yet lightweight, composite structure when welded together. The architect selected the final dimension, shape, and spacing of the alternating dimples—which acknowledge the bubble concept at a detail level— in consultation with the structural engineer and building contractor. On the interior, the steel plates are coated with a ceramic-based white paint, which smoothes sharp transitions and softens the light. The exterior is made of Corten steel, which imparts vivid color and texture to the facade.

OPPOSITE: Interior galleries
TOP LEFT: Facade of dimpled
Corten steel
TOP RIGHT: Exterior view
showing main entrance

BOTTOM LEFT: Detail of
Corten steel
BOTTOM RIGHT: Detail of
interior wall showing
ceramic paint

93

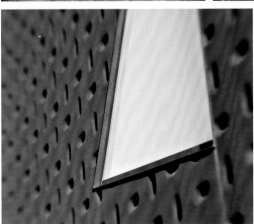

METAL

Ar de Rio Bar

Vila Nova de Gaia, Portugal
Guedes + DeCampos
2008

Based on naturally occurring examples of hexagonal geometries found in beehives and geologic formations, composite honeycomb structures are suitable for applications requiring both strength and lightness. Engineer Norman de Bruyne patented the aluminum-honeycomb-sandwich panel in 1938, and the first all-aluminum composite panel was manufactured in 1945.[23] Contemporary manufacturers like Panelite and Design Composite offer honeycomb composite panels with light-transmitting facings for architectural-cladding applications, as seen in OMA's McCormick Tribune Campus Center (2003) at Illinois Institute of Technology.

Architects Francisco Vieira de Campos and Cristina Guedes devised a completely new scale for the honeycomb assembly, employing it structurally in their Ar de Rio Bar, situated on the Douro River alongside other buildings they had previously designed using metal. The new design was based on simplicity and maximum efficiency (strength-to-weight ratio) of materials. The project folds together structure and skin, with a steel-honeycomb structure clad with insulating glass. The nearly 16 inch (40 cm) high honeycomb sections are made of 3/16 inch (5 mm) thick material, allowing, in this project, a total span of 89 feet (27 m). Despite the structure's depth, the thinness of the material allows for comprehensive views of the surrounding waterfront.

METAL

Qingpu Pedestrian Bridge

Qingpu, China
CA-DESIGN
2008

The pedestrian bridge at Qingpu Plot-18 is located in southwest Shanghai in a neighborhood undergoing rapid development. Designed by CA-DESIGN, the bridge provides pedestrian and bicycle access between two neighborhoods of dissimilar character previously separated by a 160 foot (50 m) wide river.

Taking a cue from traditional Chinese garden architecture, the covered bridge does not extend in a single, direct line across the two sides of the river but instead forms a bent path that encourages occupants to slow down and take in views from multiple vantage points. The bridge is an inhabitable steel truss that springs from two points that differ in their horizontal and vertical alignment. The traverse path formed by the bridge results in an asymmetrical bending-moment diagram when viewed in elevation, and the steel sections of the truss vary in density based on the amount of anticipated shear stress—articulating a kind of optimized grain. The bridge's shifting horizontal and vertical planes encourage visitors to pause while traveling above the water.

METAL

Za-Koenji Public Theater

Tokyo, Japan
Toyo Ito & Associates, Architects
2009

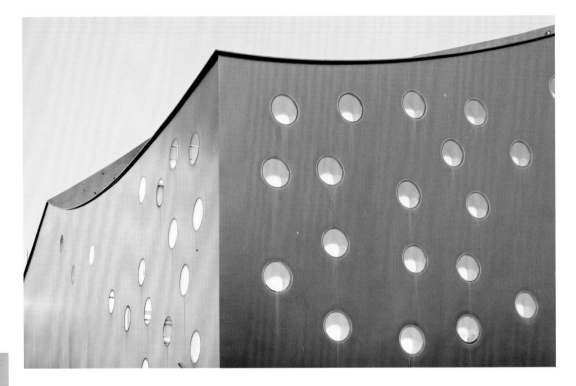

Located in Tokyo's western Suginami district, the Za-Koenji Public Theater is a center for contemporary performing arts. Artistic director Makoto Sato envisioned the project—located in a dense area composed of housing, shops, a school, and an elevated railway—as a public forum accessible to the entire neighborhood population. Designed by Toyo Ito, the building is conceived as a fixed theatrical scrim that demarcates a clear separation between the controlled environment of the theater and the frenetic activities of its site.

Ito's concept of an urban-scaled curtain, indicated by a rigid yet graceful enclosure, inspired the use of steel-and-concrete-composite cladding. This composite-facade approach continues Ito's ongoing study of monolithic structural-plate assemblies, which he has explored in his incorporation of Japanese ship-building techniques in the groundbreaking projects

such as the Mikimoto 2 building in Tokyo (2005). Ito conceived the Za-Koenji envelope as a homogeneous, multifaceted surface defined by the intersection of several catenary curves. This urban cyclorama consists of a continuous, 6 inch (15 cm) thick steel plate formed to imply seven conical and cylindrical subtractive volumes—emblematic of both a carnival tent structure and a series of gentle waves.

A series of small, round apertures perforate the Za-Koenji enclosure—another homage to marine construction. The seemingly random placement of the portholes across the facade blurs the distinction between wall and roof, and the dramatic application of interior spotlighting projects this stippled pattern onto the lobby floor. Not only does this dot motif animate the building's surfaces but also sparks the visitor's curiosity, inviting intimate connections between the building and its site.

OPPOSITE: Exterior-corner detail
TOP LEFT: Bird's-eye view

TOP RIGHT: View of interior
spiral stair from below
BOTTOM: View of interior spiral
stair from above

99

METAL

Korean Pavilion

Shanghai, China
Mass Studies
2010

"This Will Kill That" is a chapter in Victor Hugo's *The Hunchback of Notre Dame* (1831) that has long haunted architects. In it Hugo, who asserts that building was the primary mode of imparting knowledge to society (the Gothic structures of his time were laden with instructive iconography that Hugo adored), presages the replacement of the building with the book as the primary didactic medium. Since the development of the printing press, the building has been "relieved" of this responsibility, which was assumed by the written word.

The Korean Pavilion at the Shanghai Expo reimagines the role of the building as a teaching vehicle by integrating architectural form with the form of language. Designed by Mass Studies, the structure is a three-dimensional interpretation of the modern Han-Geul alphabet in scales ranging from centimeters to several stories. Two types of cladding, white laser-cut steel-composite panels and aluminum panels painted by the Korean artist Ik-Joong Kang, define the exterior and interior facades, respectively. Although the alphabet characters are arranged in abstract geometric patterns, the building communicates an elemental code complete with a miniature, simplified map of Seoul on the ground level.

Like Hugo's beloved Gothic buildings, the Korean Pavilion is completely wrapped in surfaces that communicate, albeit in an abstract way. The building explores the relationship between the language of space and the space of language, and demonstrates the extent to which verbal literacy and visual literacy are interconnected.

OPPOSITE: Exterior view
TOP: Exterior showing two
types of metal panels

BOTTOM LEFT: Facade detail
showing different sizes of
abstracted letters
BOTTOM RIGHT: Detail of
exterior panels

101

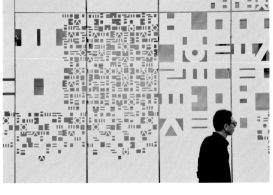

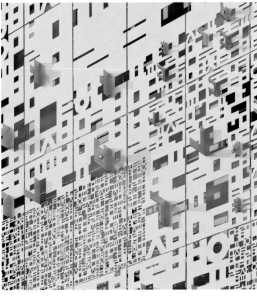

METAL

TOP: Exterior panels showing
illuminated wall cavity
BOTTOM: Detail of ground-level
courtyard

METAL

GLASS

GLASS

PAGES 104-5: Sakakura Associates, AO Aoyama, Tokyo, Japan, 2009

If we want our culture to rise to a higher level, we are obliged, for better or worse, to change our architecture. And this only becomes possible if we take away the closed character from the rooms in which we live. We can only do that by introducing glass architecture. – Paul Scheerbart

Glass is a material suspended between contradictory physical and perceptual states. Physically glass appears solid, yet it has also been called a "super-cooled liquid." In reality, it is somewhere in between a solid and a liquid—an inorganic material, called an amorphous solid, that has cooled to a rigid state without crystallization.[1] In architecture, glass is often utilized for its transparency and often regarded as immaterial; yet depending on its particular characteristics and position relative to light sources, glass can be highly reflective or opaque, with a "solidified" physical presence. Moreover, the very adoption of glass in architecture has been one of the great contradictions in building, since the incorporation of a light-transmitting and thermally inferior material may be seen to compromise the shelter and protection that is building's chief function. These divergent interpretations about glass have often resulted in robust debates about its meaning and proper use.

Given its primacy as a light-transmitting membrane in modern architecture, glass is synonymous with the concept of transparency and has been directly identified with technological progress, accessibility, democratization, and enfranchisement, as well as exposure and the loss of privacy within modern society. Although many architects treat glass as an invisible substance that allows direct connections between interior and exterior realms, others appreciate its dimensional and textural capacities to refract and suspend light rather than simply transmit it. Architectural theorists Colin Rowe and Robert Slutzky noted the contradictions inherent in the concept of "transparency as a material condition… richly loaded with the possibilities of both meaning and understanding," adding that the transparent often "ceases to be that which is perfectly clear and becomes, instead, that which is clearly ambiguous."[2] [**FIGS.1-3**]

Composition

Glass is made of pure silica (or silicon dioxide) and other additives, such as sodium oxide, calcium oxide, magnesium oxide, and aluminum oxide, that simplify processing.[3] Soda-lime glass accounts for nearly 90 percent of all manufactured glass and is roughly three-quarters silica by weight. Glass is defined as a vitreous solid formed by fusion and rapid cooling, and exists in a metastable state (a delicate condition of tentative stability) with respect to its crystalline structure.

Current glass production involves the insertion of raw materials into a gas-fired furnace, and after liquefying, the substance is refined and formed using techniques such as the float-glass method (windows) and blowing and pressing processes (jars and bottles). Glass is then typically annealed through controlled cooling in order to remove built-up stresses and may then be treated with a variety of surface procedures, lamination, or coatings for enhanced structural- and/or visual-performance characteristics. Historically, glass manufacture has often navigated various trade-offs between optical clarity, durability, and ease of processing (such as lower melting point).

TOP, LEFT TO RIGHT:
FIG. 1: Ateliers Jean Nouvel, Dansk Radio Byen, Copenhagen, Denmark, 2009, detail of glass-fin facade
FIG. 2: Kengo Kuma & Associates, Water/Glass

House, Atami, Japan, 1995
FIG. 3: Brent Kee Young, assisted by Harue Shimomoto, The Trap, 2001, detail showing colorless, flame-worked borosilicate glass

BOTTOM, LEFT TO RIGHT:
FIG. 4: Obsidian, central Mexico
FIG. 5: Example of window made with oldest mouth-blown glazing in Sweden, Kosta Glasbruk, Sweden, 1742

FIG. 6: La Sainte-Chapelle, Paris, France, 1248, detail of rose window

107

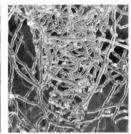

History

Glass is known to occur naturally in the silica skeletons of diatoms and in the sudden melting of earthen materials due to lightning strikes. It is also one of the oldest substances bearing the trace of human intervention, first utilized during the Stone Age in naturally occurring forms like obsidian, a volcanic glass. [**FIG. 4**] The first synthetic glass was made in Egypt and Mesopotamia, and the earliest known manufactured glass objects are beads from around 2500 BCE. Glassmaking began to flourish during the Late Bronze Age in Egypt and Western Asia, as seen in early vessels that employed the method of core-winding ductile glass ropes around a mold. Early glass objects were typically made of thin, multicolored strands that had been heated repeatedly, although glass objects were also made in a cold state with techniques borrowed from stone grinding. A popular account of glass discovery is given by philosopher Pliny the Elder, who, in *Naturalis Historia* (Natural history) (77–79 AD), describes nitrum (potassium nitrate) merchants preparing a meal on a beach: "And not having stones to prop up their pots, they used lumps of nitrum from the ship, which fused and mixed with the sands of the shore, and there flowed streams of a new translucent liquid, and thus was the origin of glass."[4]

Romans significantly advanced glass production, benefiting from the pure sand found along the Syro-Palestinian coastline. The Romans first gave glass its name—*glesum*, meaning a "transparent, lustrous material." They were also the first to use glass for architectural applications around 100 CE, and cast-glass windows began to appear in several of the most important buildings in Rome after the development of clear glass with the incorporation of manganese oxide. [**FIG. 5**] Glassmakers developed methods to color or stain glass with the addition of metallic salts, and stained glass windows may be found in Britain dating back to the seventh century. [**FIG. 6**] German glass craftspeople developed a technique to create sheet glass in the eleventh century by cutting molten glass cylinders lengthwise and laying them flat. Until the industrial revolution, glass was treated as a luxury material and only used as a major architectural element in buildings of high significance.

Modern Precedents

When tracing the use of glass in buildings from the early Middle Ages, it is possible to witness the way in which this unique material led to the dematerialization of architecture. In just the few centuries between the lofty stained-glass windows of the high Gothic style and the early conservatory buildings of the 1800s, there was a transformation in glass framing from thin stone filigree to astonishingly delicate iron tracery.

This skilled integration of glass and iron was so well executed in the construction of the massive Crystal Palace in 1851 that this building is now considered the edifice that launched the modern movement.[5] [**FIG. 7**] Designed by Joseph Paxton, the structure that housed the Great Exhibition in London was 1,851 feet (564 m) long and enclosed an interior space 108 feet (33 m) in height. The building made extensive use of prefabricated elements and ridge-and-furrow glazing, and was clad in 900,000 square feet (83,600 m²) of 16 ounce blown plate glass in only nine months.[6] The Crystal Palace was so influential that it became the symbolic exemplar of ferro-vitreous architecture, and the system of cast-iron columns, wrought-iron rails, and modular glazing became the de facto standard for large railway stations, warehouses, and market structures of the time.

Another glass structure significant to the architectural canon is Pierre Chareau's Maison de Verre (House of glass), constructed from 1928 to 1932 in Paris. [**FIG. 8**] Unlike the dematerialized quality of ferro-vitreous cladding, Maison de Verre's walls were made of translucent glass bricks, allowing substantial light transmission while maintaining privacy for the occupants of the house and doctor's office below. The skilled integration of glass bricks and steel—which resulted in a mysterious lanternlike effect at night when lit from inside—has captured the imaginations of architects for generations. The Maison de Verre provided a literal example for Le Corbusier's concept of a *machine à habiter* (machine for living) and exhibited a building-enclosure system designed to harness light rather than to simply transfer it.

No historical appraisal of modern architectural glass would be complete without reference to Philip Johnson's Glass House, the residence the architect designed for himself in 1949 in New Canaan, Connecticut. [**FIG. 9**] Inspired by the Glasarchitektur ideas developed by German architects in the 1920s and often compared to Mies van der Rohe's Farnsworth House, the Glass House surprised the American public by completely revealing the private activities of the home. Although its transparency is largely symbolic (the house is sheltered from the public eye on a large estate), this disruptive application proposed a newly ambiguous visual domain for architecture: from the inside, the surrounding environment effectively becomes the enclosure; from the outside, the see-through house is a frame that floats within the garden.

Environmental Considerations

The raw materials used to make glass are widely

available—indeed, the principal ingredient, silica, is the most abundant mineral in the earth's crust. [**FIG.10**] However, pure white silica is the preferred variety, and its repositories are subjected to greater levels of mining. Lime, used in soda-lime glass, is also highly abundant and obtained from limestone or chalk.

Additives used to make glass also have environmental ramifications. Aluminum oxide, used to improve chemical durability, requires energy-intensive processing of bauxite ore. Although silicon dioxide is inert and harmless, inhaling very fine dust can lead to lung irritations such as silicosis and bronchitis—most likely an occupational hazard for people working with sandblasting equipment. Inhalation of magnesium-oxide fumes is also dangerous and can cause metal-fume fever.

Like many building-construction materials, glass requires a large supply of energy for its manufacture. Silica has a melting point of over 1,700°C, although common additives can bring this threshold down to 1,200–1,600°C.[7] The combination of furnaces and ovens utilized for glass fabrication—as well as the energy required for transporting the product—result in energy consumption as high as two tons of carbon dioxide per one ton of glass (or 12.7 MJ/kg of embodied energy). A new generation of highly efficient ovens and controlled transportation practices (serving only local markets) promise to improve this figure. [**FIG.11**]

Glass is highly recyclable, and the means to recycle postindustrial and postconsumer glass are well established. Repurposed-waste glass is called cullet and is used to make a variety of products such as concrete countertops and industrial abrasives. However, cullet comes primarily from recycled bottle glass and not from other sources such as construction glass, which typically end up in landfills. Moreover, because preference is given to transparent glass, colored glass is not often recycled. New waste-limiting practices on building-construction sites and improved markets for a wider variety of glass types promise to increase the percentage of cullet used in future glassmaking.

By far the largest and most contentious environmental issue related to architectural glass concerns energy consumption in buildings. Despite the advances made in the energy efficiency of insulated glazing units (IGU)—which trap inert and insulating gases such as argon, krypton, or xenon between two or three panes of glass—glass remains the weak link in the thermal envelope of most buildings. As a result, modern energy codes typically stipulate the maximum percentage area that can be occupied by windows on building facades—with direct design consequences. [**FIG.12**]

The outcome is a common and predictable struggle between architects and building occupants (who desire greater light and views) against code officials and building owners (who seek reduced energy use). Moreover, environmental-rating systems, such as LEED, directly tie the mechanical-engineering performance of an entire building to its facade—minute gains in insulation value and reductions in solar-heat gain in the glass can result in significant energy

GLASS

FIG.13: Yoshio Taniguchi, Kasai Rinkai Park, Tokyo, Japan, 1995, detail of View Point Visitor's Center

FIG.14: Bubble Glass with embedded vector graphics by padLAb

FIG.15: SentryGlas Expressions digital-imaging technology by Pulp Studio, applied at the Glass Bridge Canopy by Teresita Fernández, Olympic Sculpture Park, Seattle, Washington, 2007

FIG.16: Steven Holl Architects, University of Minnesota School of Architecture, Minneapolis, Minnesota, 2002, detail of insulated structural-channel glass

 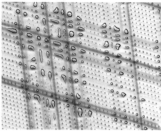  

savings over the lifespan of a structure. Further complicating this struggle is the increased (and welcome) use of operable-glazing units, which breach the external envelope and introduce outside ventilation into highly controlled interior environments.

Disruptive Technologies

The technological evolution of glass has followed two primary—and conflicting—paths. One path has been the manufacture of glass that is as perfectly immaterial as possible by reducing geometric deformities, chromatic aberrations, and surface abnormalities to imperceptible levels. [**FIG.13**] This goal is evident, for example, in large, flat storefront windows made of optically clear glass with an antireflective coating. A second avenue has been the pursuit of a wide variety of formal, structural, and aesthetic possibilities in the material—an aim that gives preference to experimentation over perfection, and substance over transparency.

Reinforcing the former tendency, new titanium-enriched coatings can provide glass with self-cleaning abilities. This technology gradually breaks down organic residue on the surface of glass with a special pyrolytic coating. In the presence of rain, the water sheets off the surface of the glass, removing dust particles and inorganic dirt so that windows dry without spots and streaks—thus enhancing the transparency of the material and reducing maintenance costs.

The latter propensity is embodied in glass products that exhibit various geometric patterns and multifaceted surfaces, and prioritize substance

over transparency. These manifestations of glass are typically designed to filter, manipulate, and embody light—as opposed to merely transmitting light—and demonstrate the vigorous research underway related to enhancing the substantive qualities of glass. One example incorporates digital-graphic content by a process of air entrainment. [**FIG.14**] The method begins with the digital incision of the desired vector graphic into sheets of glass, which are layered and then fused into a uniform panel, inevitably trapping controlled air bubbles in the material. Manufacturers have also developed computer-controlled digital-imaging systems for decorative glass, which use UV-resistant inks for many more color and image-resolution options than conventional ceramic fritting. [**FIG.15**]

Glass has also been modified to perform under greater stresses. Fire-resistant glass, for example, is made of multilaminated safety glass separated by clear intumescent layers. In the event of a fire, the intumescent layers turn opaque and expand to form an insulating heat shield, blocking the transmission of radiated and conducted heat. The layers and seals provide an integral barrier against smoke, flames, and hot toxic gasses. Glass may also be laminated with high-strength interlayer materials or cast in dimensional profiles like channels in order to accommodate additional loads safely. [**FIG.16**]

Given the intensifying pressures for the improved energy and daylighting performance of building envelopes, the most sophisticated new architectural glass products incorporate both active and passive technologies to reduce solar-heat gain,

FIG.17: Luna phosphorescent cast glass by Architectural Systems, Inc.

FIG.18: OMA, Seattle Public Library, Seattle, Washington, 2004, interior view of solar-control curtain wall

FIG.19: Foster + Partners, Willis Faber and Dumas Headquarters, Suffolk, United Kingdom, 1974

111

mitigate thermal transfer, harvest energy, as well as provide illumination and/or heating. [**FIG.17**] Electrochromic glass (also called smart glass) is a well-known technology that can alternate between transparent and opaque states with the addition of an electrical current. One version incorporates a thin film of magnesium-titanium alloy to make a switchable mirror that can easily be transformed between reflective and transparent states. This glass is intended to reduce energy consumed by air-conditioning systems in buildings and automobiles by more than 30 percent. Other examples of electrified treatments include the incorporation of low-voltage LED lighting for nighttime illumination as well as conductive interlayers designed to transform glazing into heat sources for winter thermal control.

A substantial proportion of glazing on buildings faces direct sunlight during the day and requires the use of shading or blinds. Power-harnessing glass incorporates a thin layer of solar-photovoltaic film that absorbs energy while also protecting against glare. Specialized energy-harvesting coatings and films allow windows to operate as large-area monolithic solar-cell structures. Other glazing systems designed to reduce solar-heat gain incorporate fixed microcellular shading devices that may be fine-tuned to their particular facade orientation—as seen in the curtain wall of OMA's Seattle Public Library (2004), which utilizes expanded aluminum interlayers to reduce solar radiation and glare. [**FIG.18**]

Disruptive Applications

German novelist Paul Scheerbart's 1914 *Glasarchitektur* (Glass architecture) manifesto articulated the aspirations of a burgeoning number of architects determined to replace the solidity and weight of traditional masonry buildings with the transparency and lightness afforded by glass. Bruno Taut, Mies, and other influential modern architects were inspired by Scheerbart's vision of ephemeral, crystalline structures that could transform the rigid established structure and disposition of European cities.

A century later it is possible to see the realization of Scheerbart's visions. The glass curtain wall is now the routine cladding system for commercial structures, and architects continue to seek the replacement of various opaque and structural materials with glass for the sake of increased transparency and accessibility—not to mention provocation. Norman Foster has long been a champion of structurally innovative glass architecture, as seen in his early 1974 Willis Faber and Dumas Headquarters project in Suffolk, United Kingdom. [**FIG.19**] James Carpenter has also contributed many daring architectural applications of glass, such as his 2002 Moiré Stair Tower in Bonn, Germany.

The development of high-strength glass and advanced interlayer laminations has allowed the substitution of steel, concrete, or wood with glass-based systems in small-scale structures. Notable examples include Design Antenna's Broadfield House Glass Museum (1994) in Kingswinford, Dewhurst Macfarlane and Partners' Yurakucho Canopy (1996)

TOP, LEFT TO RIGHT:
FIG. 20: Dewhurst Macfarlane and Partners, Yurakucho Canopy, Tokyo International Forum, Tokyo, Japan, 1996, detail of glass fin connection

FIG. 21: Jun Aoki, Louis Vuitton Roppongi Hills, Tokyo, Japan, 2003

BOTTOM, LEFT TO RIGHT:
FIG. 22: Herzog & de Meuron, Prada Aoyama, Tokyo, Japan, 2004

FIG. 23: Kengo Kuma & Associates, Tiffany Ginza, Tokyo, Japan, 2008

at the Tokyo International Forum, and Perkins Eastman's TKTS Booth (2008) in New York. [**FIG. 20**]

Architects have countered this pursuit of transparency by experimenting with layers of glass oriented in surprising ways. The walls of Kruunenberg Architects' Laminata Glass House (2002) in Leerdam, the Netherlands, for example, are made of thirteen thousand layers of face-mounted glass sheets of thicknesses ranging from 4 inches (10 cm) to 5 feet 7 inches (170 cm) and from nearly transparent to almost opaque. Jun Aoki's facade for Louis Vuitton Roppongi Hills (2003) in Tokyo consists of twenty-eight thousand 4 inch (10 cm) diameter transparent-glass tubes that are 12 inches (30 cm) long sandwiched between two plates of glass, creating a luminous depth unusual for a curtain wall. [**FIG. 21**]

Architects also realize visions of crystalline membranes of geometric complexity, as in Herzog & de Meuron's Prada Aoyama store (2004) in Tokyo, which utilizes curved as well as flat glazing units placed on a diagonal lattice structure. [**FIG. 22**] Resembling a faceted diamond setting, Kengo Kuma & Associates' Tiffany Ginza (2008) in Tokyo exhibits a continuously shifting surface of 292 individually mounted glass panels tilted at different angles. [**FIG. 23**]

Color is also a powerful design element in glass construction. The cladding of the Inotera Headquarters (2004) by tec Design Studio in Taipei features panels of color-printed glass in various sizes, resembling an abstract rendition of an ashlar wall. UNStudio's La Defense building (2004) in Almere, the Netherlands, makes use of 3M dichroic films, which reflect different color hues depending on the viewing angle. [**FIG. 24**].

Blue Glass Passage

Seattle, Washington
James Carpenter Design Associates Inc.
2003

Long-held assumptions about the fragility and immateriality of glass have resulted in its limited use in particular load-bearing architectural applications. However, this inherently tenuous quality has provoked architects and engineers to push the limits of glass as a structural material. The use of glass as a walkable surface elevated above a void, for example, is a highly disruptive application of the material, and results in notable visual and behavioral effects.

James Carpenter's Blue Glass Passage is a glass bridge suspended prominently over the main lobby of the Seattle city hall building. The 66 foot (20 m) long glass bridge maximizes the views of Puget Sound and the Olympic Mountain range beyond made available by the strategic siting of the building, and connects the city-council chambers with the mayor's office and administrative work spaces. The design team minimized the thickness of the glass floor to evoke a slice of blue water of the Sound. The 2¼ inch (5.72 cm) thick translucent floor plane is a laminated glass assembly that incorporates a protective ionoplast interlayer made by DuPont. This SentryGlas Secure interlayer technology was developed for high-performance seismic and security applications, and bonds well to a wide range of materials.

The resulting bridge presents an experience that challenges the senses. The first time one approaches the passage—which Carpenter describes as a "bar of captured light, floating through the lobby"—there is a moment of doubt. In place of a substantive, opaque floor hovers an aqueous plane lacking obvious supports. As the visitor travels across the bridge, his or her silhouette shifts across the lobby floor below.

OPPOSITE: View of bridge from below
TOP LEFT: View of bridge spanning building lobby

TOP RIGHT: View looking to the south
MIDDLE: Plan

BOTTOM LEFT: Passage, fabrication of laminated-glass panels

BOTTOM MIDDLE: Delivery of glass panels to the construction site
BOTTOM RIGHT: Detail showing guardrail

115

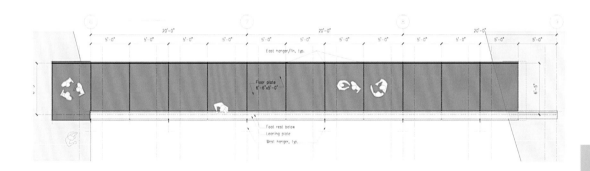

Glass Pavilion, Toledo Museum of Art

Toledo, Ohio
SANAA
2006

One of Louis Kahn's principle organizing strategies was the separation of servant and served spaces. This approach, for him, enhanced the organizational clarity of architecture by allowing the service zones to act as "insulation" between served spaces. At SANAA's Glass Pavilion of the Toledo Museum of Art, these service zones are laid bare between planes of clear glass.

A stand-alone extension that houses the Toledo Museum of Art's sizable glass-art collection, the 76,000 square foot (7,060 m²) pavilion includes spaces for a demonstration hotshop and for temporary exhibitions. Like many of SANAA's works, the project developed from a simple parti yet was complex in its realization. The pavilion diagram is a single-story "room" sandwiched between two horizontal planes, the ground plane and a thin roof. While the pavilion is physically subdivided into programmatic spaces, it is visually open because of the predominant use of floor-to-ceiling glass walls— particularly appropriate given the content of the museum. With the exception of two galleries, a small court, and two service cores, the visual territory of

the building is a single, continuous field that unites individual rooms as well as the building's exterior and interior spaces.

The Glass Pavilion employs a remarkably clever envelope strategy to avoid the energy inefficiency expected from a glass building: by utilizing two layers of insulating glass separated by an interstitial space, the envelope effectively becomes an inhabitable insulated glazing unit (IGU) that provides superior thermal control. This cavity is also supplied with radiant heating and cooling in order to optimize thermal performance.

The use of 13 foot (4 m) tall, curved, low-iron laminated glass is an exceptional application of the material. Not only does the building offer a heightened degree of visual access, but it also reveals the qualities of glass that can be enlivened by movement. As one's viewing angle changes, one's perception of the glass continually transforms between vastly different degrees of transparency, reflection, and opacity—simultaneously imparting aqueous clarity, luminous radiance, and inexplicable depth.

OPPOSITE LEFT: Interior view from the foyer
OPPOSITE RIGHT: Transparent service zone

LEFT: Interior glass walls and gypsum-board ceiling
TOP RIGHT: Northeast corner
MIDDLE RIGHT: Interior glass walls with minimal ceiling reveals

BOTTOM RIGHT: Interior showing multiple optical properties of glass

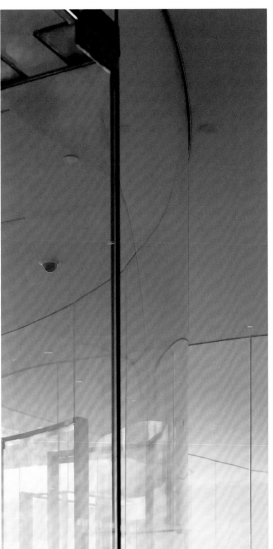

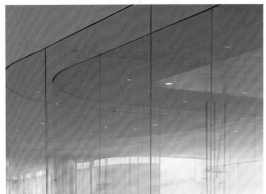

40 Bond Street

New York, New York
Herzog & de Meuron
2007

The nineteenth-century masonry-clad structures that dominate lower Manhattan are emblematic of the qualities that Paul Scheerbart desired to erase: opacity, stoutness, and immutability. The rectilinear array of vertically oriented punched windows set in thick stone or brick frames is a familiar construction language that is gradually being replaced by the taut surface of the glass curtain wall.

However, in Herzog & de Meuron's design for 40 Bond Street, glass is not applied according to the expected standards of contemporary curtain-wall construction but as a substitute for the cladding materials used in the older envelope configuration. The ten-story residential building features transparent glass windows, but the glass panes are inserted within a bulbous, infill frame (similar to older masonry buildings) of translucent green glass. To achieve the desired profile, the frame glass was cast in a bell-shaped mold and a graduated ceramic frit was applied to its surface to control light transmission. The glass was also treated with a hydrophobic, self-cleaning coating that repels dirt with the assistance of rainwater.

Herzog & de Meuron's glazing approach—which encapsulates a concrete structural frame in a window wall—contrasts markedly from the thin glass-curtain walls of Midtown skyscrapers; however, the building is also clearly distinct from its stone-faced neighbors in the East Village. 40 Bond Street represents the emergence of Scheerbart's vision—a transmutation of the old order into the new one, frozen at the moment of hesitation.

OPPOSITE: View of primary
elevation
TOP: Glass-windows and
glass frame

BOTTOM LEFT: View from interior
showing cast-glass frame
BOTTOM RIGHT: Oblique view of
the glass frame

119

Nelson-Atkins Museum of Art addition

Kansas City, Missouri
Steven Holl Architects
2007

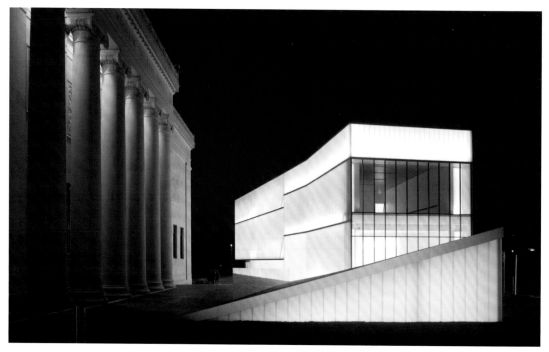

Throughout his architectural career, Steven Holl has been suspicious of transparency, preferring instead to use translucent and opaque materials. Given the usual application of glass as a transparent medium, Holl's use of translucent channel glass for the facade of the Nelson-Atkins Museum of Art addition is initially surprising. However, the glass enclosure of the museum is designed specifically to hold light rather than merely transfer it. Composed of six thousand vertically oriented, interlocking planks of low-iron channel glass with translucent insulation infill, the facade is a pellucid curtain in which light is captured and held in suspension. The exterior envelope has an additional layer of translucent laminated glazing in order to create an interstitial zone containing a 3 foot (1 m) wide service catwalk. Fluorescent light fixtures located inside this space transform the building into a softly radiating lantern at night and dissipate the murky shadows of the building's structure within.

OPPOSITE TOP: View of addition at night
OPPOSITE BOTTOM: interior with translucent channel-glass wall

TOP: Multiple architectural "lanterns" set on the landscape
BOTTOM LEFT: Exterior wall at dusk

BOTTOM RIGHT: Internally illuminated channel-glass facade

121

GreenPix

Beijing, China
Simone Giostra & Partners
2008

Designed by Simone Giostra & Partners and constructed prior to the 2008 Summer Olympics in Beijing, GreenPix explores the multifunctional, multitemporal capacities of the glass curtain wall. Described by the architects as "the first zero-energy media wall," Greenpix harnesses solar energy by day and emits programmed illumination at night.

GreenPix bridges the traditional separation between building systems and the facade, taking advantage of a cooperative pairing of sun shading and the renewable energy generated by photovoltaic cells. Glazing that receives direct sunlight is subject to solar-heat gain, and protective strategies such as ceramic fritting, tinting, or the application of reflective films reduce the intensity of solar radiation.

The modular, expandable facade system employs an integrated combination of laminated glazing, photovoltaic cells, and low-resolution-LED lighting, as well as storage batteries and hardware controllers for lighting programs. Integrated sensors allow for dynamic interaction with pedestrian movement at street level, and custom software regulates the display of live video content on the facade.

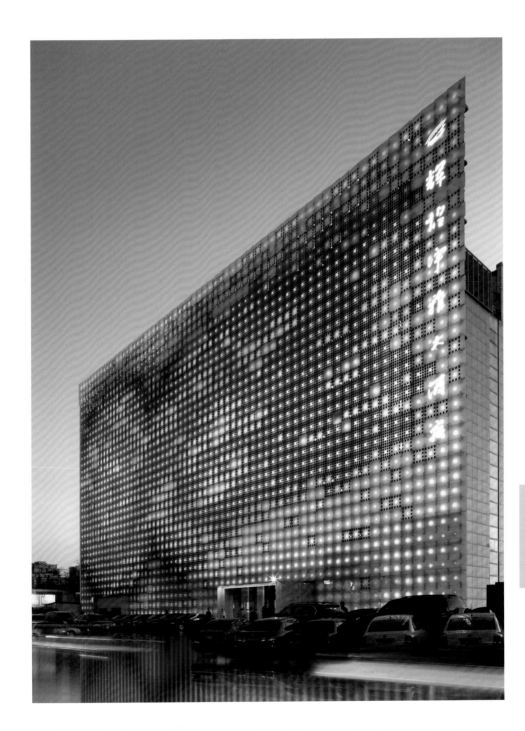

124　**TOP LEFT:** Light-intensity simulation
MIDDLE LEFT: Testing the lighting system

RIGHT: Isometric of photovoltaic-glazing modules

BOTTOM: LED illumination in different colors

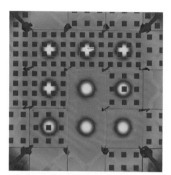

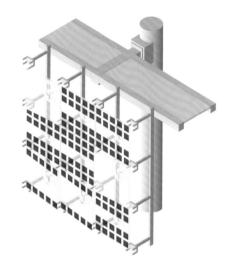

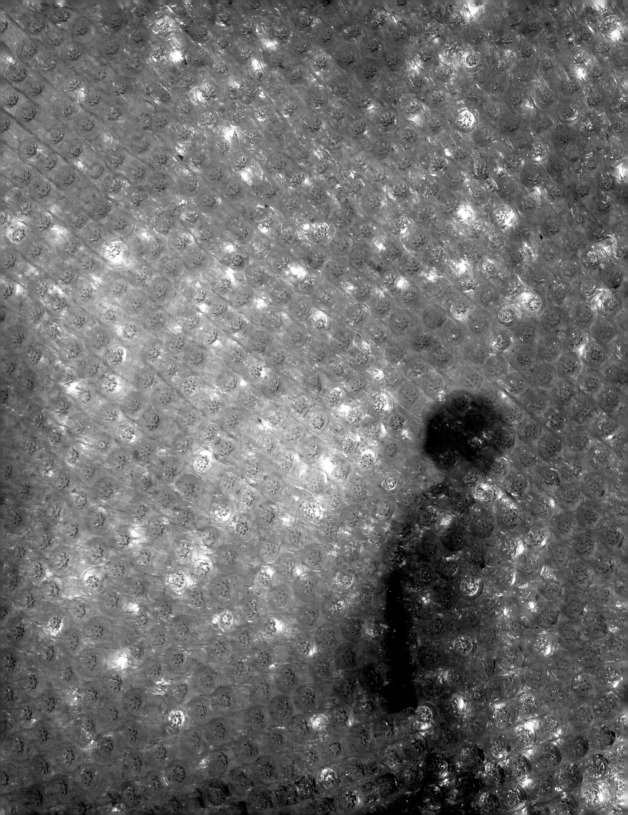

PLASTIC

PLASTIC

PAGES 126-27: Transstudio, PET Wall, Ann Arbor, Michigan, 2008

More than a substance, plastic is the very idea of its infinite transformation; as its everyday name indicates, it is ubiquity made visible. And it is this, in fact, which makes it a miraculous substance: a miracle is always a sudden transformation of nature. Plastic remains impregnated throughout with this wonder: it is less a thing than the trace of a movement. – Roland Barthes

Plastic is material born out of desire. What we describe as a synthetic polymer inherited its name from an action. The Greek verb *plassein* means "to mold or shape a soft substance" and the adjective *plastikos* refers "to something capable of being molded or shaped."[1] As chemists developed modern polymers with unprecedented and customizable properties in the twentieth century, the word *plastic* became associated with the fruits of the human impulse to manipulate material.

Plastic embodies the dilemma of the modern technological agenda. On one hand, it fulfills our aspirations for convenience, control, adaptability, and preservation; on the other hand, its production and dissemination have damaged the environment, increased the complexity of material recycling, and challenged established definitions of authenticity. Plastic is a material that endures—a desirable property by any technocentric measure—yet it does so in defiance of natural processes. Moreover, its common use as a cheap simulacrum for materials that decay has engendered distrust and ambivalence in society. Novelist Thomas Pynchon bemoaned plastic's "slick persistence;" and Toyo Ito, in lamenting the vapidity of contemporary culture, compared it to transparent cellophane: "Although we are surrounded by a variety of goods, we are living in thoroughly homogeneous atmospheres. Our affluence is supported only by a piece of Saran-wrap film."[2]

Nevertheless, plastic is a compelling material with expanding applications in architecture, and it has only begun to fulfill its technological and environmental potential. [FIG.1] Additionally, a profound shift is currently underway to replace plastic's primary feedstock of petroleum with renewable resources. As carbohydrates (renewable materials) increasingly supersede hydrocarbons (fossil fuels), plastic may one day achieve the elusive coupling of maximum control and environmental sustainability.

Composition

Produced by the conversion of raw materials into new chemical substances, plastics exhibit a wide range of characteristics—broad enough to inspire an editor from *Modern Plastics* to remark that "cellulose acetate, polystyrene, phenolics, ureas, and many other [plastic] materials are as different from each other as iron, steel, copper, or lead."[3] Plastics largely derive from fossil fuels and consist of long repeating chains of units called monomers—hence the name polymer. Plastics are typically subdivided into four categories: thermoplastics, thermosets, elastomers, and thermoplastic elastomers (TPE). Thermoplastics can be heated and cooled repeatedly and molded into complex shapes. Thermosets are typically casting resins and may only be cured once, as their polymer chains form permanent cross-links. [FIG.2] Elastomers are highly resilient plastics best described as synthetic rubber. TPES describe a hybrid category of elastomers that may

FIG.1: Lars Spuybroek, D-Tower, Doetinchem, the Netherlands, 2004

FIG.2: Dale Chihuly, Crystal Tower, Tacoma, Washington, 2002, detail of "polyvitro" (polyurethane) crystals

FIG.3: Bakelite rotary-dial phone

FIG.4: Yukinori Yanagi, Banzai Corner 96, Benesse House Museum, Naoshima, Japan, 1991, detail of mass-produced plastic figurines

129

   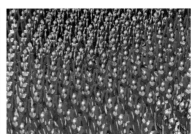

be processed like thermoplastics. Bioplastics, which are plastics derived from natural, renewable sources, are sometimes classified as their own category, although bioplastics also exhibit properties found in the other categories of synthetic plastics.

In manufacturing, plastics are commonly obtained in pellet form from industry suppliers. These pellets are mixed with additives such as fillers, colorants, flame retardants, or reinforcing materials in what is called compounding. This mixture then enters the forming process, which includes techniques such as injection molding, compression molding, rotational molding, extruding, or calendering (passed through rollers at high temperature or pressure). The most common plastics in use globally are polyethylene (PE), polyvinyl chloride (PVC), polypropylene (PP), and polyethylene terephthalate (PET), in that order.[4] In addition to PET, PVC, PP, and low- and high-density PE, the plastic industry's resin-identification code system, which identifies the different classes of plastic for recycling, includes numbers for polystyrene (PS) and "other," which is typically polycarbonate (PC) or acrylonitrile butadiene styrene (ABS).

History

Plastics were first produced in the mid-nineteenth century as a result of experiments conducted to improve the properties of natural materials. Eventually these new substances would be heralded as replacements to more expensive and flawed materials. Celluloid, invented in 1855 by British chemist Alexander Parkes and considered the first

thermoplastic, was intended to simulate tortoiseshell and amber. Bakelite, developed in 1907 by Belgian chemist Leo H. Baekeland from a mixture of coal tar–derived phenol and formaldehyde, was the first thermoset as well as one of the first plastics created from synthetic materials. [FIG.3] Bakelite was used as a surrogate for hard rubber and shellac, and found a useful application in insulating electrical components.

An explosion in plastics production occurred in the decade after 1930, which brought urea formaldehyde, polymethyl methacrylate (PMMA), polystyrene, cellulose acetate, and other synthetic polymers into commercial development. By this time plastic was a household material throughout the United States. In 1941 the British chemists V. E. Yarsley and E. G. Couzens declared the "Plastic Age" to be "already upon us," and described the futuristic life of Plastic Man, who would be born "into a world of color and bright shining surfaces, where childish hands find nothing to break, no sharp edges or corners to cut or graze, no crevices to harbor dirt or germs." Plastic now emanated a utopian atmosphere, and was predicted to create "a world free from moth and rust and full of color."[5]

Plastic also had its detractors. The surge in plastic products available after World War II came to be associated with the newfound materialism of the era, and many considered plastic to be a shallow and artificial material.[6] [FIG.4] Polytetrafluoroethylene (PTFE), PET, and low- and high-density PE were also in full production. The full test of plastics, such as Bakelite and polyethylene, by the military during

FIG. 7: Fuller, United States
Pavilion, detail of dome
enclosure

  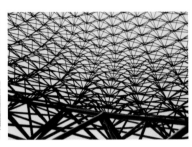

World War II helped convince skeptics of their full potential—no longer mere conversation pieces, plastics had demonstrated their capabilities under the most demanding circumstances. Plastic thus became a pervasive material in automotive, furniture, toy, and clothing manufacturing—by this time, nylon had been developed as a replacement for silk and neoprene for rubber—completely transforming these industries as a result.

Modern Precedents

Although initial applications of plastic tended to favor small, mass-produced objects, the development of building-scaled plastic systems intensified during the late 1950s. Plastic fabricators were able to make plastics that could accommodate the large scale of buildings with newly developed methods such as lamination and glass-fiber-reinforced molding. Early plastic architecture was generally envisioned in one of two ways: rigid forms made of molded panels or tension-based structures made of flexible fabrics. The latter category consisted of both tent structures and inflatable structures.[7]

Albert Dietz was a structural engineer credited with realizing the Monsanto House of the Future in 1957. [**FIG. 5**] Dietz's Plastics Research Laboratory at Massachusetts Institute of Technology (MIT), which helped develop nylon-based armor during World War II, was approached by Monsanto in 1954 to research and design an innovative house. In search of plastic's unique expression, Dietz and architectural associate Richard Hamilton decided on a total facade enclosure

for the house, defined by a continuous plastic surface. Designed with mass production in mind, the House of the Future assumed the form of four joined cantilevered pods elevated on a central plinth. The C-shaped pods were made of glass-fiber-reinforced polyester, fabricated in L-shaped bents and lowered into position by crane on-site. Although news reports made the installation seem effortless, the construction process was laborious, messy, and required significant manual labor to finish properly.

Buckminster Fuller's interest in factory-built housing after the war led to an interest in the geodesic dome, a modular construction that provided maximum volume with a minimal material surface area. Fuller's earliest small domes, which were built at MIT, were self-supporting structures with thin metal struts clad with lightweight materials. His design for the United States pavilion at the 1967 Montreal Expo consisted of an almost completely spherical dome, 200 feet (61 m) tall and 250 feet (76 m) in diameter. [**FIGS. 6+7**] Clad in nineteen hundred clear molded-acrylic sheets set in neoprene gaskets on steel-pipe chords, the dome resembled "a lacy filigree weightless against the sky."[8] For Fuller, plastic offered the possibility for a nearly immaterial architecture based on complex structural patterns found in nature.

Munich's Olympic Stadium embraced this idea in a different form. [**FIG. 8**] Designed by architect Günter Behnisch and engineer Frei Otto for the 1972 Summer Olympics, the stadium featured the largest acrylic-paneled roof structure of its kind—covering nearly 860,000 square feet (80,000 m²) of area.

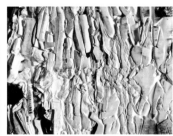

Echoing the topography of the Alps, the collection of tent structures was supported by steel suspension cables tethered to tall masts. Due to the complex geometry of the surface, the 9 foot 6 inch x 9 foot 6 inch (2.9 x 2.9 m) rigid acrylic panels, which are $^5/_{32}$ inch (4 mm) thick, were designed to float above neoprene pedestals attached to a 29½ x 29½ inch (75 x 75 cm) steel-cable net. Requiring extensive structural calculations prior to construction, the intricate structures hover like giant transparent umbrellas above an expansive landscape.

Environmental Considerations

Synthetic plastic is derived from fossil fuels, and it shares many of the criticisms of oil and gas—including the depletion of nonrenewable resources, contribution to global warming, emission of pollutants, and augmentation of the global competition for petroleum, which, unfortunately, lends support to so-called petro-dictatorships. [**FIG. 9**] However, plastics utilize oil more wisely than fuel, since heat can be recovered from plastics when they are melted down for fuel at the end of their product life. Plastic feedstock accounts for only about 4 percent of global oil production, and another 4 percent is used as energy in plastics manufacturing. Moreover, recycled and renewable feedstocks have the potential to reduce the dependence on fossil fuels in plastic manufacturing.

Many plastics emit toxins during some stage of their life. During manufacturing or when burned, PVC releases dioxin, a known carcinogen. Polyurethane (PUR) contains diisocyanates; urea and melamine contain formaldehyde; and polyester and epoxy contain styrene.[9] Some plastics release volatile organic compounds (VOC), or off-gas, into the atmosphere during much of their life, contributing to respiratory problems. Bisphenol A (BPA) and phthalates used to make certain plastics are known endocrine disruptors, and even small quantities have been shown to cause developmental problems in the human body. These chemicals have already been spread widely throughout the environment and do not decay readily. Efforts must be made to reduce or eliminate the use of these substances, as well as employ necessary safety precautions during manufacture.

Although plastic's defiance of natural decay is a positive quality during its useful life, this durability is not always desirable, particularly given its enduring visibility in the environment when not disposed of properly. [**FIG. 10**] Ten percent of waste plastic finds its way to the world's oceans, and sea currents have aggregated the materials into five different gyres—floating islands of lasting refuse that create environmental dead zones.[10] Fortunately, thermoplastics are easily recyclable if they are discarded properly, and thermosets may be reground to make new composites (although this is not common). Making new plastics with recycled material also reduces embodied energy, and one ton of recycled plastic can save up to 685 gallons of oil, resulting in a 50 to 90 percent savings over the energy used to make virgin plastic.[11] It is therefore important to consider the recyclability and disassembly of plastic components during the design and specification process.

PLASTIC

Increasingly, bioplastics are being developed with the intent to replace petroleum with natural, renewable feedstocks. [**FIG.11**] The most common bioplastics are polylactides (PLA), made from natural lactic acid harnessed from corn or milk, and poly-hydroxyalkanoates (PHA, PHB), produced from the fermentation of sugars or lipids in soybean oil, corn oil, or palm oil.[12] While bioplastics are primarily used for disposable products like packaging, containers, and bottles, they are gradually being utilized for more demanding applications such as casings and microprocessors for mobile electronic devices, automobile-body parts, and building-construction materials. These latter uses typically require the brittle bioplastics to be modified with plasticizers and reinforced with glass or kenaf fibers. In addition to requiring less energy to produce, bioplastics are also biodegradable. Depending on the particular chemistry used to make a bioplastic, it is possible to program its longevity appropriately for its function.

Disruptive Technologies

Because it is a relatively novel material, plastic is closely associated with the idea of contemporary society. It has had a visible role in the development of modern technology and culture, and it remains a controversial material. Technological advances in plastic generally follow two paths: performance enhancement and material substitution. Performance enhancement delivers materials that are lighter, stronger, more durable, supple, or colorfast than other materials, while material substitution refers to plastic's use as a simulacrum for other substances. Given heightened concerns about the imperishability of discarded plastic, a third technological trajectory now addresses the responsible reuse of plastic waste in new materials and the creation of bioplastics that safely biodegrade.

Originally developed for truck beds, durable and lightweight plastic-composite-honeycomb panels are being used for architectural applications with greater frequency. These panels consist of a structural honey-comb core made of polycarbonate or aluminum sandwiched between two solid polymer sheets, such as fiberglass or cast-polyester-resin facings. The high stiffness, low weight, and light transmission of these polymer composites make them appropriate for light-duty structural applications, such as walls, flooring, and work surfaces, especially considering the wide range of colors and finishes available.

Performance enhancement not only suggests mechanical and aesthetic improvement but also involves self-regulation and response—the criteria for smart materials. A self-healing polymer is a structural polymeric material with the ability to autonomically heal itself. [**FIG.12**] Inspired by biological systems, self-healing plastics incorporate a catalytic chemical trigger and a microencapsulated healing agent within an epoxy matrix. Developing fissures rupture the micro-capsules, releasing healing agent into cracks through capillary action.

Responsive plastics include shape-memory poly-mers, which can change from a rigid state to an elastic one and back, allowing the potential for configurable architecture, furniture, molds, packaging, and so on.

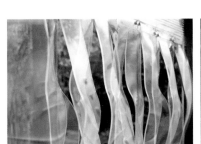

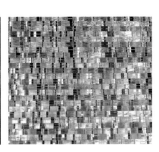

[**FIG.13**] These materials can be readily manipulated once heated above their activation temperature and will hold this new shape indefinitely until heated again—at which time they will return to their original cured shape. One outcome of research in responsive surfaces is a polymer-based window that regulates both light and ventilation and changes shape by opening and closing gill-like slats, increasing airflow when air quality decreases below ideal levels. [**FIG.14**]

Plastic is commonly used in digital-fabrication methods, such as 3-D printing. Scientists have developed engineered nanocomposite resins specifically for such processes, in which objects are constructed by depositing sequential layers of polymer that are cured to form a rigid object—a process called additive manufacturing. The MIT Media Lab has experimented with photopolymer composites printed with OBJET's Polyjet matrix technology, allowing for the realization of complex geometries with two polymers that assume different mechanical roles—such as structure and skin—based on their physical properties. Another technique called three-dimensional multiphoton lithography, developed by the Georgia Institute of Technology, uses a focused laser beam to cure polymer gel to a solid.

Plastic also contributes to the availability of renewable energy. Organic photovoltaics (OPV) are polymers used to conduct electricity and harness energy. Despite their relative inefficiency, OPVs are popular due to their ability to be produced in large volumes at low cost. Lightweight, flexible films made of multiple nanostructured layers of OPV convert light to energy for a wide variety of applications. Because the films are sensitive to a broader light spectrum than conventional solar cells, they derive power from all visible light sources. Flexible and lightweight OPV-based energy-harvesting systems are easily mounted to existing building facades to add low-cost renewable-energy capability.

Emerging polymer technologies explore new and unexpected effects of light propagation, since plastic readily transmits and filters light. Polymer light emitting diodes (PLED) emit light in the presence of an electrical charge. Initially developed at Cambridge University in 1989, PLEDs are highly efficient and enable the fabrication of thin lighting displays with superior clarity, brightness, visibility from a wide viewing angle, and manufacturing simplicity compared to liquid-crystal displays (LCD).

Plastic-mirror film was designed to maximize the efficiency of light transmission. Although it is completely polymer-based, polymer film can exhibit over 99 percent light reflectance—more than any metal. [**FIG.15**] It also reflects color more accurately than silver or aluminum, which are the most common metals used to make mirrors. The film is used in daylight-delivery systems to extend the reach of sunlight into dark interiors. Other notable materials include polyester films that transform between transparent and translucent states based on the viewing angle, antireflective films inspired by the eye structure of night-flying moths, and structured-polymer panels that utilize a three-dimensional matrix of light pipes to transmit light into dark areas. [**FIG.16**]

PLASTIC

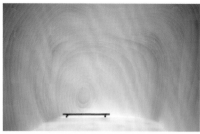

Since its creation plastic has been used as a surrogate for other materials. Versions of ivory, lacquer, cotton, wood, stone, and metal have been rendered convincingly in plastic—although touch typically reveals the true identity of the material. Although this substitution has largely been driven by economic interests, there are other motivations. DuPont's Corian, for example, is a solid surfacing material used in place of stone or quartz. Made of acrylic and alumina trihydrate, the material was originally developed to replace human bones in medical research. Its durability, malleability, and impermeability make Corian superior to other solid surfacing materials.

Polymers made from corn and other primary agricultural sources have made possible a wider variety of renewable resource–based plastics, including chitinous polymers derived from mushrooms that are designed to replace balsa wood, kenaf fiber–reinforced bioplastics for computer and mobile-phone casings, as well as soybean and chicken-feather composites used to make circuit boards. [**FIG.17**]

Impending shortages of petroleum and the inescapable plastic-disposal problem have inspired the creation of plastics made from reused materials, and a growing number of companies produce a variety of sheet products from recycled plastic waste. Crushed discarded compact discs, PC water bottles, translucent milk jugs, PS food packaging, PP-based carpet, and polyester cassette tape are just a few polymer materials that resourceful manufacturers now regularly repurpose into new products.

Disruptive Applications

Plastic is inherently a disruptive material in architecture. The development of synthetic polymers has led to the replacement of an increasing number of construction materials with plastic surrogates. Piping, siding, windows, waterproofing, wall covering, furniture, and various coatings and adhesives all have plastic variants that have replaced products made of wood, stone, ceramics, and metal in common construction. This displacement phenomenon is largely based on economic incentives, as plastic products are often designed to simulate the materials they have replaced at lower cost.

Early polymer chemists recognized the public perception of plastics as inferior and sought to strengthen the tenuous image of plastic—they declared polymers no longer "substitute materials," but substances created "by man to his own specifications."[13] Indeed, plastics have been developed with unique sets of properties that reinforce their particular identities. Most of the plastics used in contemporary building were invented between 1931 and 1938, and intensive development of architectural applications began in the late 1950s and continues today.[14]

One growing trend involves the use of lightweight structured panels for walls and apertures. Sheet materials of PMMA or PC in plain, corrugated, or multiple-layered configurations have become popular due to their lightness, light-transmitting capabilities, and insulation potential. Kengo Kuma & Associates' Plastic House (2002) in Tokyo is clad in

 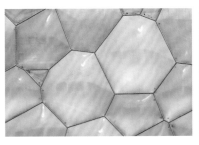  

an assembly of translucent-PC panels fastened on either side of light-gauge steel channels and translucent sheet insulation. The firm's ethereal Oribe Tea Pavilion (2005) in Tajimi, Japan, makes use of closely spaced corrugated plastic sheets that are connected by plastic inserts, eliminating the need for steel supports. The result is a dreamlike space that resembles a light-emanating cocoon. [**FIGS.18+19**]

Similar to the use of panels in the Plastic House, Nendo's Book House (2005) in Tokyo is clad in translucent fiber-reinforced-plastic (FRP) panels that, from inside, subtly reveal the shadows of books located on exterior shelves. Other projects using lightweight structured-plastic panels include SOMOS Arquitectos' Vallecas 51 project (2009) in Madrid, which employs colored-PC panels on an operable aluminum-curtain-wall system, and Moomoo Architects' Lo1 House (2008) in Lodz, Poland, which uses insulating plastic composite panels as exterior cladding.

Some of the most influential applications of plastic have celebrated its sculptural potential. Early projects like the Monsanto House of the Future and Matti Suuronen's mass-produced Futuro Haus (1968) in Finland have inspired successive generations of architects to embrace both formal and performance opportunities of plastic. Lars Spuybroek is a visible proponent of plastic as a sculptural medium, as seen in projects such as his *D-Tower* (2004) in Doetinchem, the Netherlands—a 39 foot (12 meter) tall installation with a structural-polymer surface that emits multiple colors at night. (See page 129, figure 1.)

Other architects have exploited plastic's apparent softness. SANAA's Dior Omotesando building (2004) in Tokyo, for example, makes use of semitransparent, rigid acrylic "curtains" to create a gossamer skin behind the exterior glass. [**FIG.20**] Plastic has demonstrated desirable environmental-performance benefits when used as a textile-based envelope system for large structures, such as the air-inflated ETFE cladding of Nicholas Grimshaw & Partners' Eden Project (2001) in Cornwall, United Kingdom, and PTW's Beijing National Aquatics Center for the 2008 Summer Olympics. [**FIG.21**] Plastic-based textiles have also been employed widely in noninflated, taut skins, such as in the glass fiber–reinforced PVC curtains in Jean Nouvel's Copenhagen Concert Hall (2009), which is a brightly colored scrim by day and projection screen at night. [**FIG.22**]

Architects have also invented second-life applications for plastics. Atelier FCJZ developed an unexpected additional function for the plastic pavement blocks typically used to reinforce ground cover in parking areas, specifying them instead for the walls and the roof of the Plastic Outhouse (2005) in Beijing. [**FIG.23**] During construction these structured-honeycomb modules were connected together to make larger surfaces that were clad on both sides with translucent polycarbonate sheets. Recycled-PET beverage containers were assembled into interlocking modules in Transstudio's PET Wall (2008), a self-supporting, translucent light curtain that aggregates injection-molded plastic modules to form an expansive light-diffusion lens. (See pages 126–27.)

PLASTIC

Armani Fifth Avenue

New York, New York
Massimiliano & Doriana Fuksas
2009

Harrison Abramovitz & Abbe's 1959 Corning Glass building—the Fifth Avenue address where Armani commissioned a flagship store—is a respected example of the International Style. When Massimiliano & Doriana Fuksas embarked on the store's design, they deferred to the original building's facade and instead concentrated their energies on a distinct interior experience.

The focus of the 43,000 square foot (3,995 m²) store is a grand staircase that links three stories inside a 45 foot (13.7 m) tall space. The stair connects the entire retail area in one fluid, uninterrupted volume. Made of rolled-plate steel with a seamless white-polymer coating, the stair forms a complex, intertwined geometrical vortex. The lack of visible supports, combined with the abstract quality of the smooth resin finish, creates the illusion that the stair defies gravity. LED-light tape installed on the bottom surface of the handrails accentuates the sweeping line of the treads.

The plastic-clad stair-sculpture celebrates the fundamental spirit of plasticity. Defined by motion itself, the stair conforms to the imprint of the designer's will—like frozen liquid suspended in a phantasmagoric void.

TOP: Ground-level view
of grand staircase
BOTTOM: Detail of stair
geometry

Learning from Nature Pavilion

Humlebaek, Denmark
3XN
2009

For the 2009 Green Architecture for the Future exhibition, Denmark's Louisiana Museum of Modern Art invited 3XN to design a pavilion that would explore the frontiers of sustainable and intelligent materials. Despite the pavilion's intimate dimensions of approximately 26 x 16 x 11½ feet (8 x 5 x 3.5 m), the architects imbued it with large-sized ambitions. Because many green materials fulfill only a single environmental purpose, 3XN wanted to develop a new composite that would assimilate a broad array of functions, including power generation, phase-change capability (the ability to store and release large amounts of energy), rapid renewability, recyclability, self-cleaning, and illumination.

The result was a Möbius strip delineated by a single, curvilinear plane made of a new biocomposite of flax fibers, cork, and a corn-and-soybean-derived bioresin. The architects wanted a plastic material that would be made of rapidly renewable, naturally harvested resources that would safely biodegrade

at the end of the pavilion's life. The cork and flax fibers are coated with Envirez, the first commercially available unsaturated-polyester resin made from renewable and recycled content.

3XN embellished their biocomposite with additional technologies, including microspheres of phase-changing materials that store latent heat, which maintains a comfortable surface for seating despite temperatures that change throughout the day. A thin, glassy coating containing titanium dioxide nano-particles and another coating made of nanostructured silica provide pollution reduction and self-cleaning functionality. Piezoelectric sensors located on the lower region of the strip also derive energy from pressure exerted by touch, which powers LED lights in conjunction with flexible solar-photovoltaic film installed on the top surface. The outcome is a decep-tively simple sculptural installation that explores an alternative future for plastic and inspires learning and interaction within its context.

OPPOSITE: The pavilion installed at the Louisiana Museum of Art with the harbor beyond
TOP: View looking back toward the museum.

BOTTOM LEFT: Raw materials used to make the biocomposite
MIDDLE AND BOTTOM RIGHT: Fabrication of the pavilion structure

PLASTIC

City Code

Shanghai, China
Natalija Miodragovic and Darko Kovacev
2010

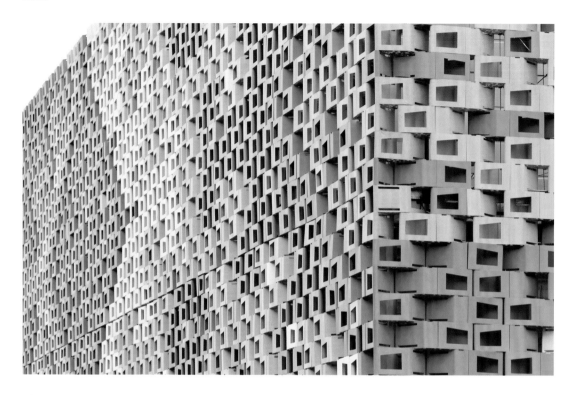

The carpet-weaving method called *čilim* is a centuries-old tradition originating from the southeastern Serbian town of Pirot. The industry is led by women who produce intricate, multicolored carpets and tapestries entirely by hand using a reversible flat-weave technique. The painstakingly woven textiles incorporate various vivid motifs from both Islamic and Christian traditions, contributing to their easy recognition and visual appeal.[15]

Given the importance of the čilim technique to their cultural heritage, the Serbian architects Natalija Miodragovic and Darko Kovacev used it as inspiration for their design of the Serbian pavilion, City Code, at the 2010 Shanghai Expo. The weaving tradition, to Miodragovic and Kovacev, symbolizes unification, and the synthesis of materials is a metaphor for cultural harmony.

Each čilim carpet has its own unique, hand-crafted pattern—a condition the architects interpreted as code. Miodragovic and Kovacev translated various čilim patterns in the application of an abstract architectural system on the building's facade. They developed wedge-shaped recycled PP blocks, called Serboxes, in several colors to represent the weft fibers, and the blocks were suspended on a grid of steel cables representing the warp strands. The cellular wedges were alternated and stacked in order to construct a pattern without repetition that wraps the building, in a kind of unpredictable code. The polymer blocks feature trapezoidal apertures that add visual depth as well as space for internal lighting, and their radiused edges ensure seamless transitions at building corners. Moreover, the Serboxes were designed for post-expo use as containers or furniture for the storage or transport of goods.

OPPOSITE: Facade showing
the formation of čilim patterns
TOP: Modules internally
illuminated

BOTTOM LEFT: Entrance
at night
BOTTOM LEFT: Oblique
view of facade

143

Media-TIC

Barcelona, Spain
Cloud 9 (Enric Ruiz Geli)
2010

Enric Ruiz Geli's bold design for a new *mediatheque* in the expanding 22@Barcelona district is a digital-community hub for media entrepreneurs and information-technology companies. Located in the former nucleus of nineteenth-century Catalan industry, the 249,000 square foot (23,104 m²) building represents the transformation of an industrial epicenter into a hub for the information economy.

The design of Media-TIC was inspired by two local sources: the district's nineteenth-century factories and Antonio Gaudí's celebrated Casa Milà (1912), located in the Eixample neighborhood. The boxlike Media-TIC's uniform truss structure is reminiscent of the cathedrals of industry, while its expressive facade recalls the flamboyance of Gaudí's architecture.

The building is wrapped in ETFE cladding designed to regulate solar-heat gain and glare. Each of the self-cleaning ETFE "pillows" possesses up to three air chambers that inflate according to need: one is transparent and the other two have patterns that when overlapped completely block out sunlight. Under normal conditions the system allows for the transmittance of light and views, but with direct sun exposure, the pneumatic system shifts to the second and third layers to create shade. In keeping with passive-solar principles that acknowledge different levels of solar exposure on different parts of the facade, no two sides of the building are alike. The most exposed south-west facade is equipped with lenticular tubes of ETFE filled with nitrogen. These "vertical clouds" automatically fill with liquid nitrogen during the hottest hours of the day, acting as a smoke screen for direct rays.

The combination of a bold long-span structure and environmentally tuned facade make the Media-TIC a highly flexible building for the digital operations housed within. For Ruiz Geli, it is a performative architecture that embodies the shifting terrain of information.

OPPOSITE: South-east facade
TOP: Facade cavity

BOTTOM LEFT: Detail of ETFE
system reflected in window
BOTTOM RIGHT: Detail of
south-east facade with ETFE
cladding

145

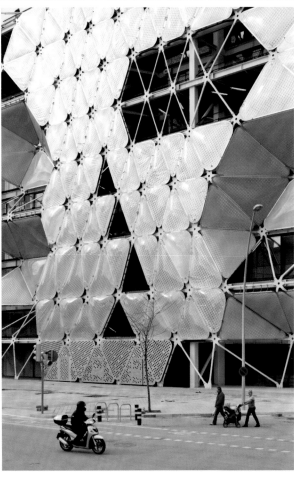

Seed Cathedral

Shanghai, China
Heatherwick Studio
2010

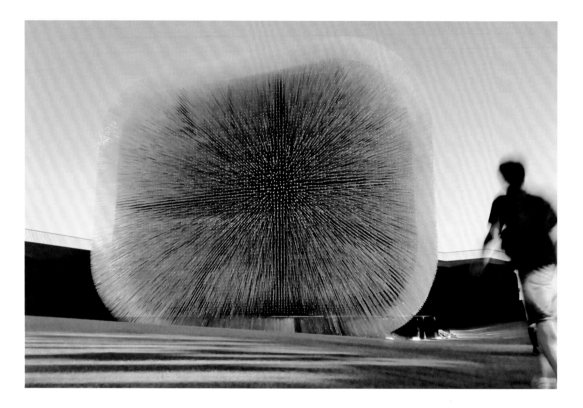

Heatherwick Studio's UK Pavilion for the Shanghai Expo 2010 is a visually arresting structure that appears to be caught in a moment of emergence—or disappearance. Covered with sixty thousand projecting, light-transmitting acrylic rods, the pavilion design seeks to expand the territory of the architectural facade. In photographs as well as in person, the soft, delicately delineated edges of the building appear more like a rendering than reality—a result of Heatherwick's purposeful blurring and thickening of the envelope.

The 64,600 square foot (6,000 m²), 66 foot (20 m) tall Seed Cathedral presents visitors with a rich variety of seeds collected from the Kew Gardens' Millennium Seed Bank Project in Surrey, United Kingdom. The pavilion's undulating, womblike interior is shaped by the ends of the 24 foot 7 inch (7.5 m) long optical strands that extend outward, each of which has a seed embedded in its tip. Deep behind the tips of the rods is the building's structure, which consists of a steel-and-wood diaphragm embedded with aluminum sleeves into which the filaments are inserted. The sleeve holes were located and drilled with great accuracy using a CNC-milling machine with spatial information from a three-dimensional CAD file.

During the day the interior space is illuminated by sunlight propagated through the rods; at night the exterior subtly glows from the activation of inconspicuously embedded light sources. As the wind stirs, the pavilion's deep facade responds by gently moving its thousands of cilia.

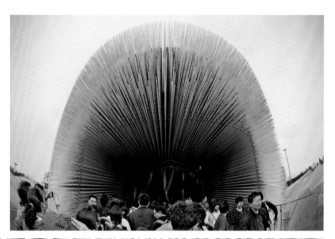

TOP: View showing the expanded spatial territory of the facade
BOTTOM: Detail of exterior rod connection

TOP: Interior ceiling
BOTTOM: Interior detail of acrylic
rods with embedded seeds

149

Image Credits

21. Kazushi Takahashi, interviewed by Takafumi Suzuki, "Crossbreeding Shipbuilding with Architecture," trans. Claire Tanaka, *Pingmag*, July 7, 2008, http://pingmag.jp/2008/07/07/crossbreeding-shipbuilding-with-architecture/.
22. Ibid.
23. Tom Bitzer, *Honeycomb Technology: Materials, Design, Manufacturing, Applications and Testing* (London: Chapman & Hall, 1997), 3.

Glass
The epigraph to this chapter is drawn from Paul Scheerbart, *Glasarchitektur*, as translated in Dennis Sharp, ed., *Glass Architecture by Paul Scheerbart; and Alpine Architecture by Bruno Taut*, trans. James Palmes (*Glass Architecture*) and Shirley Palmer (*Alpine Architecture*) (Santa Barbara, CA: Praeger, 1972), 41. *Glass Architecture* was originally published as *Glasarchitektur* (Berlin: Verlag Der Sturm, 1914).
1. Clara Curtin, "Fact or Fiction? Glass Is a (Supercooled) Liquid" in *Scientific American*, February 22, 2007, http://www.scientificamerican.com/article.cfm?id=fact-fiction-glass-liquid.
2. Colin Rowe and Robert Slutzky, "Transparency: Literal and Phenomenal," in *The Mathematics of the Ideal Villa and Other Essays* (Cambridge, MA: MIT Press, 1976), 160–61.
3. Hegger, Auch-Schwelk, Fuchs, and Rosenkranz, *Construction Materials Manual*, 85.
4. Pliny the Elder's account in Georgius Agricola, *De re metallica* (*On the Nature of Metals*), trans. Herbert Clark Hoover and Lou Henry Hoover (Mineola, NY: Dover Publishing, 1950), 586.
5. Wigginton, *Glass in Architecture*, 10.
6. Ibid., 42.
7. Hegger, Auch-Schwelk, Fuchs, and Rosenkranz, *Construction Materials Manual*, 85.

Plastic
The epigraph to this chapter is drawn from Roland Barthes, *Mythologies* (New York: Noonday Press, 1972), 97.
1. Jeffrey L. Meikle, *American Plastic: A Cultural History* (New Brunswick, NJ: Rutgers University Press: 1995), 4.

2. Thomas Pynchon, *Gravity's Rainbow* (New York: Viking Press: 1973), 600–601; and Toyo Ito, "Architecture in a Simulated City," *El Croquis* 71 (1996): 13.
3. Stephen Bass, "The Plastics Industry Has Come of Age," *Modern Plastics* 23 (April 1946): 132.
4. Michael F. Ashby, *Materials and the Environment* (Burlington, MA: Butterworth-Heinemann, 2009), 17.
5. V. E. Yarsley and E. G. Couzens, "The Expanding Age of Plastics," *Science Digest* 10 (December 1941): 57–59.
6. Meikle, *American Plastic*, 6.
7. Thomas Herzog, Roland Krippner, and Werner Lang, *Facade Construction Manual* (Basel: Birkhäuser, 2004), 211.
8. Sylvia Hart Wright, *Sourcebook of Contemporary North American Architecture: From Postwar to Postmodern* (New York: Van Nostrand Reinhold, 1989), 33.
9. Rob Thompson, *Manufacturing Processes for Design Professionals* (New York: Thames & Hudson, 2007), 429.
10. Ed Fitzgerald, "Pacific Ocean Plastic Waste Dump," *Ecology Today*, August 14, 2008, http://ecology.com/ecology-today/2008/08/14/pacific-plastic-waste-dump/.
11. "Recycling Trivia," Mississippi Department of Environmental Quality, accessed April 9, 2011, http://www.deq.state.ms.us/Mdeq.nsf/page/Recycling_RecyclingTrivia?OpenDocument.
12. Ashby, *Materials and the Environment*, 310–12.
13. "A Little Cotton and a Little Camphor Make You This Finer Fountain Pen!," *DuPont Magazine* 32 (midsummer 1928), advertisement, inside front cover.
14. Herzog, Krippner, and Lang, *Facade Construction Manual*, 211.
15. Laurence Mitchell, *Serbia* (Buckinghamshire, UK: Bradt Travel Guides, 2007), 313.

Front cover: Fernando Guerra
Back cover: Christian Richters
6–7: top Daici Ano

Mineral
14–15: Daici Ano
18: left (FIG. 6) Andreas Überschär
19: top left (FIG. 10), top right (FIG. 11) Marissa Fabrizio; bottom left (FIG. 12), bottom middle (FIG. 13) Christine Spetzler; bottom right (FIG. 14) Lisa Tsang
20: top left (FIG. 15), top middle (FIG. 16), top right (FIG. 17) Eric E. Olson; bottom left (FIG. 18) M. F. Wills; bottom right (FIG. 19) Friðrik Bragi Dýrfjörð
21: top right (FIG. 22) Brembo
22: left (FIG. 23) Benjamin Cook/E-Green Building Systems; middle (FIG. 24) Fraunhofer IKTS Dresden; right (FIG. 25) Keith Carlson/Photo-Form LLC
23: left (FIG. 26), middle left (FIG. 27) Studio Gang Architects
24: David Mézerette
25: top David Mézerette; bottom left Genppy; bottom right Xiaohei Black
26–27: Daici Ano
28: top, middle right, and bottom right Kengo Kuma & Associates; bottom left Daici Ano
29: Daici Ano
30: Gramazio & Kohler/Ralph Feiner
31: Gramazio & Kohler
32: Adam Mørk
33: top and middle Adam Mørk; bottom left, bottom right 3XN
34–35: Adam Mørk

Concrete

44: (FIGS. 7–9) Doris Lohmann
45: left (FIG. 10), middle left (FIG. 11) Xavier de Jauréguiberry; middle right (FIG. 12), right (FIG. 13) Tadao Ando Architects & Associates
46: left (FIG. 14) Macau500; middle (FIG. 15) CANMET; right (FIG. 16) AltusGroup
47: left (FIG. 17) Rieder Faserbeton-Elemente GmbH; middle (FIG. 18) Victor Li; right (FIG. 19) Italcementi
48: left (FIG. 20) Meld USA; middle left (FIG. 21) SensiTile Systems; middle right (FIG. 22) Brandon Shigeta
50: Bart van den Hoven
51: top Bart van den Hoven; middle left, middle right Norbert Heyers; bottom left, bottom right Bart van den Hoven
52–53: Áron Losonczi
54–55: Benoît Fougeirol
56: Hélène Binet
57: top Roland Halbe; bottom Hélène Binet
58–59: Sandra Draskovic

Wood

64: top left (FIG. 7), top middle (FIG. 8), top right (FIG. 9) Anthony V. Thompson; bottom left, bottom right (FIGS. 10+11) Alvar Aalto Foundation
65: left (FIG. 12) Anthony V. Thompson; middle (FIG. 13) Dustin Holmes
66: left (FIG. 15) Pete Nichols; middle (FIG. 16) Jaksmata; right (FIG. 17) Architectural Systems, Inc.
67: left (FIG. 18) John Christer Hoiby; middle (FIG. 19) Reholz GmbH; right (FIG. 20) Architectural Systems, Inc
68: left (FIG. 21) Terry Bostwick Studio Furniture; right (FIG. 23) German Nieva
69: top left (FIG. 24) Satoshi Asakawa; bottom left (FIG. 26) Gramazio & Kohler, Architecture and Digital Fabrication, ETH Zurich
70–71: William Pryce
72–73: Iwan Baan
74: Carlos Tavella
75: top, bottom left Ned Baker; bottom right Carlos Tavella

Metal

87: middle (FIG. 11) Nat Hansen; right (FIG. 12) Piero Russo
88: left (FIG. 13) Sydney Pollack; middle (FIG. 14) Geomartin; right (FIG. 15) U.S. Fish and Wildlife Service
89: left (FIG. 16) Cellular Materials International, Inc.; middle (FIG. 17) Fraunhofer Institute
90: left (FIG. 19) Haresh Lalvani; middle (FIG. 20) Intaglio Composites
91: top right (FIG. 24) Daici Ano
92: Daici Ano
93: top left, top right Daici Ano
92–93: Fernando Guerra

Glass

107: top middle (Fig. 2) Mitsumasa Fujitsuka; bottom middle (Fig. 5) Mogens Engelund; bottom right (Fig. 6) Didier B
108: left (FIG. 7) Royal Horicultural Society; middle (FIG. 8) Subrealistsandu; right (FIG. 9) Lisa Tsang
109: left (FIG. 10) Jim Gordon
110: middle left (FIG. 14) Penny Herscovitch
111: left (FIG. 17) Architectural Systems, Inc.; right (FIG. 19) Nigel Young/Foster + Partners
113: (FIG. 24) Christian Richters
114: Brian Gulick
115: top left, top right, bottom right Brian Gulick; middle, bottom left, bottom middle James Carpenter Design Associates Inc.
118–19: Iwan Baan
120–21: Andy Ryan
122–25: Simone Giostra and Partners-ARUP-Ruogu

Plastic

129: left (FIG. 1) NOX/Lars Spuybroek; middle right (FIG. 3) Louise Docker
130: left (FIG. 5) Charles R. Lympany
131: left (FIG. 8) Michael Kieltyka; middle (FIG. 9) Erik Christensen
132: left (FIG. 11) Natureworks LLC; middle (FIG. 12) Magnus Andersson; right (FIG. 13) NEC Corporation
133: left (FIG. 14) The Living; middle (FIG. 15) Caleb Nelson; right (FIG. 16) SensiTile Systems
134: left (FIG. 17) Center for Composite Materials, University of Delaware; middle (FIG. 18), right (FIG. 19) Daici Ano
135: left (FIG. 20) Laurie McGinley; right (FIG. 23) Atelier FCJZ
136: Ramon Prat
137: Massimiliano & Doriana Fuksas
138: top Ramon Prat; bottom Massimiliano & Doriana Fuksas
139: Ramon Prat
140: Adam Mørk
141: top Adam Mørk; bottom left Steven Achiam
142: middle, bottom right Stage One
144–45: Iwan Baan